Praise for the new edition of
Winning the Loser's Game

"The best book about investing? The answer is simple: *Winning the Loser's Game*."

—F. William McNabb III, Chairman, President,
and CEO, The Vanguard Group, Inc.

"A must-read classic that has stood the test of time—both in the markets and on the courts."

—Martin Leibowitz, Managing Director
at Morgan Stanley Research

"This remarkably insightful and lucidly written investment classic should be required reading for every serious investor."

—Burton G. Malkiel, author of
A Random Walk Down Wall Street

"The first edition of Charley Ellis's great *Winning the Loser's Game* was published in 1985. Each subsequent edition has gotten more comprehensive, and more timely, and his seventh edition is best of all. Read it. Enjoy it. Learn from it."

—John C. Bogle, Founder of the Vanguard Group
and First Index Mutual Fund

"This is by far the best book on investment policy and management."

—Peter Drucker

"As a rookie reporter in the 1980s, I read a slim book with an unassuming title: *Investment Policy*. It's simple but powerful message changed the way I thought about investing. Today, *Investment Policy* is called *Winning the Loser's Game*. It's considered an investment classic, and deservedly so. For those who have never enjoyed the wisdom of Charley Ellis, a treat awaits you."

—Jonathan Clements, author of *How to Think About Money*
and founder of HumbleDollar.com

"A must-read. This clearly written book explores concepts essential to both institutional and individual investors. It is not a simplistic 'do-it-yourself ' cookbook, but an elegant guide to investment truths and paradoxes."

—**Abby Joseph Cohen,** Stock Market Strategist and
Managing Director, Goldman, Sachs & Co.

"Radical in its simplicity. Investors—institutional and otherwise—will find this jolt to their cherished beliefs refreshing."

—**Adam Smith,** author of *Adam Smith's Money World*

"An outstanding guide for the individual investor, full of sound and useful advice for making one's way through the confusing maze of our contemporary financial world."

—**William E. Simon,** former Secretary of the Treasury

"No one understands what it takes to be a successful investor better than Charley Ellis and no one explains it more clearly or eloquently. This updated investment classic belongs on every investor's bookshelf.

—**Consuelo Mack,** Executive Producer and
Managing Editor, *Consuelo Mack WealthTrack*

"This is less a book about competition than about sound money management. Sounder than Charley Ellis they do not come."

—**Andrew Tobias,** author of *The Only
Investment Guide You'll Ever Need*

"Ellis has written a liberating book about investing. This book will enable you to face your money matters squarely, with intelligence and vision, and help you create a plan that will increase the security and freedom of your later years"

—**Byron R. Wien,** Morgan Stanley

WINNING
THE LOSER'S
GAME

SEVENTH EDITION

TIMELESS STRATEGIES
for SUCCESSFUL
INVESTING

CHARLES D. ELLIS

New York Chicago San Francisco Athens London Madrid
Mexico City Milan New Delhi Singapore Sydney Toronto

1 2 3 4 5 6 7 8 9   QFR   22 21 20 19 18 17

ISBN   978-1-259-83804-0
MHID   1-259-83804-8

e-ISBN   978-1-259-83805-7
e-MHID   1-259-83805-6

This publication is designed to provide accurate and authoritative information in regard to the subject matter covered. It is sold with the understanding that neither the author nor the publisher is engaged in rendering legal, accounting, securities trading, or other professional services. If legal advice or other expert assistance is required, the services of a competent professional person should be sought.
> —*From a Declaration of Principles Jointly Adopted by a Committee of the American Bar Association and a Committee of Publishers and Associations*

Library of Congress Cataloging-in-Publication Data

Names: Ellis, Charles D., author.
Title: Winning the loser's game : timeless strategies for successful investing / Charles D. Ellis.
Description: Seventh edition. | New York : McGraw-Hill, [2017] | Includes index.
Identifiers: LCCN 2016055006 (print) | LCCN 2017005411 (ebook) | ISBN 9781259838040 (alk. paper) | ISBN 1259838048 | ISBN 9781259838057 () | ISBN 1259838056
Subjects: LCSH: Portfolio management. | Investments. | Investment analysis.
Classification: LCC HG4529.5 .E45 2017 (print) | LCC HG4529.5 (ebook) | DDC 332.6--dc23
LC record available at https://na01.safelinks.protection.outlook.com/?url=https %3A%2F%2Flccn.loc.gov%2F2016055006&data=01%7C01%7Ckari.black%40 mheducation.com%7Cbe42a50cc5414aa4c5f008d44ecd01d6%7Cf919b1efc0c34 7358fca0928ec39d8d5%7C1&sdata=XSiA34a%2FM3pj%2BF0NEfbMJeko2iFpdp j5HuohLXFCr%2BQ%3D&reserved=0

McGraw-Hill Education books are available at special quantity discounts to use as premiums and sales promotions or for use in corporate training programs. To contact a representative, please e-mail us at bulksales@mheducation.com.

*For Linda Lorimer, my beloved wife and best
friend. You helped me learn that striving to
maximize quantitative investment results was not
as important as assuring financial security and
the freedom to enjoy living well comfortably.*

CONTENTS

PREFACE

Lucky me! Married to a wonderful and inspiring woman, I was born in the United States; privileged in education; blessed with parents, children, and grandchildren I like, admire, and enjoy; and also blessed with an unusually wide global circle of friends in investment management—an endlessly fascinating profession in a remarkably favored business—replete with bright, engaged, and creative people.

Investing can seem way too complex, and investing wisely can take too much time. Most individuals are too busy to take the time to "learn all about it." They and you have better things to do.

With increasing concern, I've seen the long-term professionalism that attracted me to investing get increasingly compromised by short-term commercialism and investor uncertainties about how to manage investment for the long term. With all my advantages comes a clear responsibility to serve others. That's why I wrote this book.

Over the past century, the securities markets have changed massively, and in many ways, creating an overwhelming problem for individual *and* professional investors. Those profound changes are explained in Chapter 1, "The Loser's Game." Raised in a tradition that if you recognize a problem, you should look for a good solution, I've written this short book of straight talk. Each reader can understand the realities he or she faces and know how to take appropriate action to convert the usual loser's game into a winners' game in which every sensible investor can and should be a long-term winner.

As Winston Churchill so wisely observed, "People like winning very much!" We all like winning with investments, and we all can win—at lower costs, less risk, and less time and effort if we can clarify our real objectives, develop sensible long-term policies, and stick with them so the markets' fluctuations are working for us, not against us.

In over 50 years of learning about investing from outstanding practitioners and expert theorists around the world, I've tried to collect, distill, and explain clearly and as plainly as possible the principles for successful investing. For both individual investors and institutional investors who have the necessary self-discipline and wish to avoid the loser's game, the simple messages in this short book are now and will be the keys to success in the winner's game of sensible investing for the *next* 50 years.

The core principles of successful investing *never* change—and never will. Sure, the companies change, and markets and economies go up and down—sometimes a lot. In fact, when short-term data appear to be most challenging to core principles is exactly when they are most important and most needed. That's why, when you've read this book, you'll know all you really need to know to be successful in investing.

Many people—too many to name—have generously contributed to my long learning about investing. Ruth Hamel's deft editing has improved every page. She is a joy to work with and learn from. Brooke Rosati, patiently smiling and humming as we work together in our small office, has converted my hieroglyphics into consistent clear copy.

Charles D. Ellis
New Haven, CT
November 2016

INTRODUCTION

In *Winning the Loser's Game*, Charley Ellis teaches lessons valuable to investors in sparkling and engaging prose. All of us should heed his words.

Winning the Loser's Game stands in the pantheon of books for individual investors alongside Burt Malkiel's *A Random Walk down Wall Street* and Jack Bogle's *Common Sense on Mutual Funds*. In the seventh (and final?) edition of his classic, Ellis reminds us repeatedly that low-cost index funds provide the foundation for investment success and financial security.

Ellis' enthusiastic and carefully reasoned endorsement of index investing delivers a strong rebuke to the active management strategies prevalent in today's mutual fund industry. Overwhelmingly, as Ellis frequently points out, funds attempting to beat the market fail to meet their goal. Since Ellis praises the quality of the analytical work done by mutual fund portfolio managers, what is the problem?

The crux of the problem is that mutual fund managers generally fail to discharge their fiduciary responsibility to investors. Instead of putting investor interests front and center, which would require limiting assets under management to levels that might allow active management success, mutual fund managers succumb to the siren song of bloated funds that generate bloated profits.

Why is the size the enemy of performance? Larger size requires more positions. Instead of a manager's twenty best ideas, a larger fund contains the manager's fifty (or one hundred) best ideas. What is the chance that the fiftieth (or one hundredth!) best idea is a good as the twentieth? Not very high. As the size of assets under management increases, the size of the investable universe decreases. Large funds compete to win by investing in large companies that are heavily researched and efficiently priced. Smaller nimble funds have a distinct advantage in the performance derby, choosing among less heavily researched and less efficiently priced securities.

At the same time as excessive assets impede performance, they generate handsome profits for the managers. As size increases, fees increase. Expenses fail to keep pace, turning the actively managed mutual fund into a profit machine. Few and far between are the mutual funds that limit assets under management to serve investor interests.

Mutual fund managers further breach their fiduciary responsibility with extraordinarily high rates of portfolio turnover, estimated by Ellis to be in the neighborhood of 60% to 80% per year. High turnover, resulting from a futile attempt to beat the market on a short-term basis, leads to realization of gains (in our generally rising markets), which results in a tax bill for the investor. A true fiduciary would operate with a longer investment horizon or close high-turnover funds to taxable investors.

Investors want fund managers whose primary goal is to generate high returns and, in the words of one of Yale's managers, to join the rate of return hall of fame. Overwhelmingly, mutual fund managers collect excessive fees and spend their days in the rate of return hall of shame.

The conflict between fiduciary responsibility and profit motive resolves in favor of profits far more often than not. Individual investors are left holding the bag.

To address the investor's conundrum, Ellis offers the solution of low-cost index funds. Vanguard, the most prominent provider of index funds, is uniquely positioned to serve investors. Founder Jack Bogle conceived Vanguard without a profit motive, structuring the firm in a way that allowed investors to own the funds in which they invest. Bogle eliminated the conflict between fiduciary responsibility and profit motive by eliminating profits. Vanguard exists for investors. Period.

Is there a place for active management in today's market? Let me answer by telling you something about my experience as Yale's Chief Investment Officer.

When I began managing Yale's endowment in 1985, I addressed the challenge with a strong belief in market efficiency. As I terminated the hapless active mangers that predated my arrival, I redeployed the proceeds into index funds. Soon, more than half of the endowment was indexed.

Yet, Yale's move from active to index was tempered by the recognition that several managers that I inherited were pursuing sensible strategies that promised to add value to the portfolio. Intrigued, my team and I began a search for others. In a matter of years, Yale's index exposure was largely gone, replaced by high quality active managers.

Charley Ellis was at the center of the transformation of the Yale endowment. I first encountered Charley in the late 1980's when he was giving a speech to an investment management group. Charley spoke about how his education at Phillips Exeter, Yale and Harvard changed his life. He informed the group that he intended to dedicate his life to giving back to those institutions that were so important to him. I decided then and there that I wanted Charley to be part of Yale's investment program. First as an informal advisor, then as a member of Yale's investment committee from 1992 to 1998 and finally as chair of the committee from 1999 to 2008, Ellis' rock-solid wisdom and steady hand played a critical role in my professional development and Yale's investment success.

Active management of Yale's endowment portfolio has added enormous value to the university. In the past 30 years, Yale's return of 12.9% per annum far exceeded the 8.8% return of a passive portfolio of 60% U.S. equities and 40% U.S. bonds. The difference in returns added $28.2 billion of value to Yale, which came partly in the form of higher payouts to support Yale's mission of teaching and research and partly in the form of higher endowment values.

The Yale investments office added these many billions of dollars through the dedicated efforts of a world-class team of investment professionals, currently numbering 30. The investment staff scours the world, seeking investment opportunities exploited by extraordinary investors supported by individuals organized in small entrepreneurial firms. When the Yale staff identifies a potential investment manager, they roll up their sleeves and conduct extremely thorough due diligence. (One long-time Yale partner claimed the university contacted his third grade teacher for a reference.) After clearing the investigative phase, the staff then negotiates a fair compensation structure that rewards investment success. Careful monitoring follows. Nearly all of the external managers with which Yale invests are not available to ordinary investors. Without having substantial financial resources and a high quality dedicated staff, it is nearly impossible to succeed in the cutthroat world of active management.

In 2000, I published *Pioneering Portfolio Management*, which outlined my principles for managing Yale's endowment. Soon thereafter, I began my book for individual investors. Initially, I intended to adapt my portfolio management approach at Yale to the opportunity set for individual investors. As I investigated the world of investment alternatives, I realized that ordinary individuals do not have access to the options available to Yale. Reluctantly, with the 2005 publication of *Unconventional Success*, I concluded that individuals should avoid active management entirely.

The investment management world is unusual in that the correct approaches are at the extremes. Sensible investors either index everything (which is the correct approach for almost all individuals and the vast majority of institutions) or manage everything actively (which is the correct approach for only those wealthy individuals and institutions that commit extraordinary resources to achieving active management success). Unfortunately, most investors end up in the sloppy middle, paying high fees (and unnecessary taxes) for mediocre performance.

Even though I admire and heartily support Ellis' approach to investing, I have two concerns. First, I worry that Ellis underestimates the value of diversification in favor of pure equity market exposure. While he endorses various forms of equity exposure – foreign developed, foreign emerging, real estate – he suggests that investors avoid long-term investment in bonds. I prefer broader diversification. To the equity classes listed above, I would add allocations to US Treasury bonds and US Treasury Inflation Protected Securities. Ellis correctly notes that investors frequently fail to maintain equity exposure in times of market stress. He believes the solution is education and fortitude. I believe the solution is broad diversification (and education and fortitude). Second, Ellis suggests that investors, particularly younger investors, might benefit from modest amounts of borrowed money to increase the size of their portfolios. I worry that the well-documented tendency of investors to chase performance, buying after strong results and selling after poor, would be exacerbated by borrowed money, increasing the likelihood of untimely moves into and out of markets and adding to the individual investor's woes. These differences notwithstanding, I enthusiastically embrace the lessons of *Winning the Loser's Game*.

David F. Swensen
Chief Investment Officer
Yale University
New Haven, Connecticut
November 2016

CHAPTER 1

THE LOSER'S GAME

DISAGREEABLE DATA ARE STREAMING STEADILY OUT OF THE computers of performance measurement firms. Over and over again, these facts and figures inform us that most mutual funds are failing to "perform" or beat the market. The same grim reality confronts institutional investors such as pension and endowment funds. Occasional periods of above-average results raise expectations that are soon dashed as false hopes. Contrary to their often-articulated goal of outperforming the market averages, investment managers are not beating the market; the market is beating them.

Faced with information that contradicts what they believe, people tend to respond in one of two ways. Some ignore the new knowledge and hold firmly to their beliefs. Others accept the validity of the new information, factor it into their perception of reality, and put it to use. Most investment managers and most individual investors, being in a sustained state of denial, are holding on to a set of romantic beliefs developed in a long-gone era of different markets. Their romantic views of "investment opportunity" are repeatedly—and increasingly—proving to be false.

Investment management, as traditionally practiced, is based on a single core belief: investors *can* beat the market, and superior managers *will* beat the market. That optimistic expectation was reasonable 50 years ago, but not today. Times have changed the markets so much in so many major ways that the premise has proven unrealistic: in round numbers, over one year, 70 percent of mutual funds underperform their chosen benchmarks; over 10 years, it gets worse: over 80 percent underperform.

Yes, several funds beat the market in any particular year and some in any decade, but scrutiny of the long-term record reveals that very few funds beat the market averages over the long haul—and nobody has yet figured out how to tell in advance which funds will do it.

If the premise that it is feasible to outperform the market were true, then deciding *how* to go about achieving success would be a matter of straightforward logic.

First, because the overall market can be represented by a public listing such as the S&P 500 or the Wilshire 5000 Total Market Index, a successful active manager would only need to rearrange his or her portfolios more productively than the "mindless" index. The active manager could choose to differ from the chosen benchmark in stock selection, strategic emphasis on particular groups of stocks, market timing, or various combinations of these decisions.

Second, because an active manager would want to make as many "right" decisions as possible, he or she would assemble a group of bright, highly motivated professionals whose collective purpose would be to identify underpriced securities to buy and overpriced securities to sell—and, by shrewdly betting against the crowd, to beat the market. With so many opportunities *and* so much effort devoted to doing better, it must seem reasonable to casual observers that experienced experts working with superb information, powerful computer models, and great skill would outperform the market—as they so often did decades ago.

Unhappily, the basic assumption that many institutional investors can outperform today's market is false. Today, the institutions *are* the market. They do more than 98 percent of all exchange trades and an even higher percentage of off-board and derivatives trades. It is precisely because investing institutions are so numerous and capable, and so determined to do well for their clients, that investment management has become a *loser's game*. Talented and hardworking as they are, professional investors cannot as a group outperform themselves. In fact, given the operating costs of active management—fees, commissions, market impact, and taxes—most active managers will continue to underperform the overall market every year, and over the long term, a large majority will underperform.

Individuals investing on their own do even worse—on average, much worse. Day trading is the worst of all: a sucker's game. Don't do it, ever.

Before analyzing what happened to convert institutional investing from a winner's game into a loser's game, consider the profound difference between the two kinds of games. In a winner's game, the outcome is determined by the correct actions of the *winner*. In a loser's game, the outcome is determined by the mistakes made by the *loser*.

Dr. Simon Ramo, a scientist and one of the founders of TRW Inc., identified the crucial difference between a winner's game and a loser's game in an excellent book on game strategy, *Extraordinary Tennis for the Ordinary Tennis Player*.[1] Over many years, Ramo observed that tennis is not one game but two: one played by professionals and a very few gifted amateurs, the other played by all the rest of us.

Although players in both games use the same equipment, dress, rules, and scoring, and both conform to the same etiquette and customs, they play two very different games. After extensive statistical analysis, Ramo summed it up this way: Professionals *win* points; amateurs *lose* points.

In expert tennis, the ultimate outcome is determined by the actions of the *winner*. Professional tennis players hit the ball hard with laserlike precision through long and often exciting rallies until one player is able to drive the ball just out of reach or force the other player to make an error. These splendid players seldom make mistakes.

Amateur tennis, Ramo found, is almost entirely different. Amateurs seldom beat their opponents. Instead, they beat themselves. The actual outcome is determined by the *loser*. Here's how: brilliant shots, long and exciting rallies, and seemingly miraculous recoveries are few and far between. The ball is all too often hit into the net or out of bounds, and double faults at service are not uncommon. Rather than try to add power to our serve or hit closer to the line to win, we should concentrate on consistently getting the ball back so the other player has every opportunity to make mistakes. The victor in this game of tennis gets a higher score *because the opponent is losing even more points.*

As a scientist and statistician, Dr. Ramo gathered data to test his hypothesis in a clever way. Instead of keeping conventional game scores—15–love, 15–all, 30–15, and so forth—he simply counted points *won* versus points *lost*. He found that in expert tennis about 80 percent of the points are *won*, whereas in amateur tennis about 80 percent of the points are *lost*.

The two games are fundamental opposites. Professional tennis is a winner's game: the outcome is determined by the actions of the winner. Amateur tennis is a loser's game: the outcome is determined by the actions of the loser, who defeats himself or herself.

The distinguished military historian Admiral Samuel Eliot Morison made a similar central point in his thoughtful treatise *Strategy and Compromise*: "In warfare, mistakes are inevitable. Military decisions are based on estimates of the enemy's strengths and intentions that are usually faulty, and on intelligence that is never complete and often misleading. Other things being equal, the side that makes the fewest strategic errors wins the war."[2]

War is the ultimate loser's game. Amateur golf is another. Tommy Armour, in his book *How to Play Your Best Golf All the Time*, says, "The best way to win is by making fewer bad shots."[3]

This is an observation with which all weekend golfers would concur.

There are many other loser's games. Like institutional investing, some were once winner's games but have changed into loser's games with the passage of time. For example, 100 years ago, only very brave, athletic, strong-willed young people with good eyesight had the nerve to try flying an airplane. In those glorious days, flying was a winner's game. But times have changed, and so has flying. If the pilot of your 747 came aboard today wearing a 50-mission cap and a long, white silk scarf around his or her neck, you'd get off. Such people no longer belong in airplanes because flying today is a loser's game with one simple rule: Don't make *any* mistakes.

Often, winner's games self-destruct because they attract too many players, all of whom want to win. (That's why gold rushes finish ugly.) The "money game" we still call investment management evolved in recent decades from a winner's game to a loser's game because a basic change occurred in the investment environment: The market came to be overwhelmingly dominated by investment professionals—all knowing the same superb information, having huge computer power, and striving to win by outperforming the market they collectively completely dominate. No longer is the active investment manager competing with overly cautious custodians or overly confident amateurs who are out of touch with the fast-moving market. Now he or she competes with hundreds of thousands of other hardworking investment experts in a loser's game where the secret to "winning" is to lose less than the others lose, by enough to cover all the costs and fees. The central problem is clear: As a group, professional investment managers are so good that they all make it nearly impossible for any one of them to outperform the market—the expert consensus they collectively determine.

Today's money game includes a truly formidable group of competitors. Several thousand institutions—hedge funds, mutual funds, pension fund managers, private equity manag-ers, and others—operate in the market all day, every day, in the most intensely competitive way. Among the 50 largest and most active institutions, which do half of all trading, even the small-est spends $100 million in a typical year buying services from the leading broker-dealers in New York, London, Frankfurt, Tokyo, Hong Kong, and Singapore. Understandably, these formidable competitors want to get the "first call" with important new ana-lytical insights, but the Securities and Exchange Commission now requires publicly owned companies to make every effort to assure that all investors get the same useful information at the same time. Thus, almost every time individual investors buy or sell, the "other fellow" they trade with is one of those skillful pro-fessionals—with all their experience, all their information, all their computers, and all their analytical resources.

And what a tough group of skillful professionals they are! Top of their class in college and graduate school, they are "the best and the brightest"—disciplined and rational, supplied with extraordinary information by thousands of expert analysts who are highly skilled and are *all* playing to *win*.

Sure, professionals make mistakes, but the other pros are always looking for any error so they can pounce on it. Important new investment opportunities simply don't come along all that often, and the few that do certainly don't stay undiscovered for long. (Regression to the mean, the tendency for behavior to move toward "normal," or average, is a persistently powerful phenom-enon in physics, sociology, *and* investing.)

The key question under the new rules of the game is this: How much better must the active mutual fund investment manager be to at *least* recover the costs of active management? The answer is daunting. If we assume 80 percent annual portfolio turnover (implying that the fund manager holds a typical stock for 14 months, which is slightly longer than average for the mutual fund industry) and we assume average trading costs (commissions plus the impact of big trades on market prices) of 1 percent to buy and 1 percent to sell, plus 1.25 percent in mutual fund fees and expenses, the typical fund's operating costs before taxes are 3.25 percent per year.[4]

So an active manager must overcome a drag of about 3.25 percent in annual operating costs just to break even. For the fund manager to match the market's generally expected 7 percent future rate of return, he or she must return 10.25 percent before all those costs. In other words, to do merely as well as the market net, an active manager must be able to outperform the market—the consensus of experts—in gross returns by more than 46 percent![5] Achieving such superiority is, of course, virtually impossible in a market dominated by professional investors who are intensely competitive, extraordinarily well informed, and continuously looking for any opportunity to exploit.

That's why the stark reality is that most active managers and their clients have *not* been winning the money game. They have been losing. So the burden of proof is surely on the manager who says, "I am a winner; I can win the money game."

For any one manager to outperform the other professionals, he or she must be so skillful and so quick that he or she can regularly catch the other professionals making mistakes—and systematically exploit those mistakes faster than the other professionals can. (Even the pros make *macro* mistakes, particularly being fully invested together at market peaks, trying to anticipate the anticipation of the other pros, who, of course, are anticipating one another's anticipations. When they make *micro* mistakes, they correct their errors quickly or see them exploited and quickly corrected by their professional competitors.)

The reason investing has become a loser's game even for dedicated professionals is that their efforts to beat the market are no longer the most important part of the *solution*; they are now the most important part of the *problem*. As we learn in game theory, each player's strategy should incorporate understanding and anticipation of the strategies and behavior of other players. In the complex problem each investment manager is now trying to solve, his or her efforts to find a solution—combined with the efforts of many expert competitors—have become the dominant adverse reality facing all active managers.

It's not the individual active manager's fault that his or her results are so disappointing. The competitive environment within which active managers work has changed dramatically in the past 50 years from quite favorable to very adverse—and it keeps getting worse because so many brilliant and hardworking people with extraordinary equipment and access to superb information keep joining in the competition.

To achieve better-than-average results through active management, you must depend directly on exploiting the mistakes of others. Others must act as though they are *willing to lose* so you can win after covering all your costs of operation. Back in the 1960s, when institutions did only 10 percent of public trading and individual investors did 90 percent, large numbers of amateurs were realistically bound to lose to the professional active managers.

* * * * *

Working efficiently, as Peter Drucker so wisely explained, means knowing how to do things the right way, but working effectively means doing the right things. Because most investment managers will not beat the market in the future, all investors should at least consider investing in index funds so they will never get beaten by the market. Indexing may not be fun or exciting, but it works well. The data show that index funds have outperformed most investment managers. And the challenges to active managers have been getting tougher as professionals have increasingly dominated the market.

For most investors, the hardest part of "real life" investing is not figuring out the optimal investment policy; it is staying committed to sound investment policy through bull and bear markets and maintaining what Disraeli called "constancy to purpose." Being rational in an emotional environment is never easy. Holding on to a sound policy through thick and thin is both extraordinarily difficult and extraordinarily important work. This is why investors can benefit from developing and sticking with sound investment policies and practices. The cost of infidelity to your own commitments can be very high. Sustaining a long-term focus during market highs or market lows is notoriously difficult. At either kind of market extreme, emotions are strongest when current market action appears most demanding of change and the apparent "facts" seem most compelling.

An investment counselor's proper professional priority is to help each client identify, understand, and commit consistently and continually to long-term investment objectives that are both realistic in the capital markets and appropriate to that particular investor's true objectives. Investment counseling helps investors choose the right objectives *and* stay the course.

Before examining the many powerful changes in the investment world, let's remind ourselves that active investing is, at the margin, *always* a negative-sum game. Trading investments among investors would by itself be a zero-sum game, except that the large costs—as a percentage of returns—of management fees and expenses plus commissions and market impact must be deducted. These costs total in the billions of dollars every year.

Even more discouraging to investors searching for superior active managers is the evidence that managers who have had superior results in the *past* are not particularly likely to have superior results in the *future*. In investment performance, the past is *not* prologue except for the grim finding that those who have repetitively done badly are likely to stay in their slough of despair.

The one encouraging truth is that while most investors are doomed to lose if they play the loser's game of trying to beat the market through active investing, every investor can be a long-term winner. To be long-term winners, we need to concentrate on setting realistic goals and developing sensible investment policies that will achieve those objectives, and have the self-discipline and fortitude required for persistent implementation of those policies so each of us can enjoy playing a true winner's game. That's what this book is all about.

Notes

1. Simon Ramo, *Extraordinary Tennis for the Ordinary Tennis Player* (New York: Crown Publishers, 1977).
2. Samuel Eliot Morison, *Strategy and Compromise* (New York: Little Brown, 1958).
3. Tommy Armour, *How to Play Your Best Golf All the Time* (New York: Simon & Schuster, 1971).
4. More than brokerage commissions and dealer spreads are properly included in transaction costs. The best way to show how high transaction costs are is to compare the theoretical results of a "paper" portfolio with the actual results of a "real money" portfolio. Experts will tell you that the differences are impressive. And there's yet another cost of transactions: that of unwisely getting into stocks you would not have purchased if you were not "sure" you could get out at any time because the market looked so liquid. This is the real liquidity trap. Think how differently people would behave on the highway or in the bedroom if they were sure they would be caught. It's the same with investments: you don't always get caught, nor do you always not get caught. All these costs are part of the total.
5. This makes the superior performance of Warren Buffett of Berkshire Hathaway and David Swensen of Yale University all the more wonderful to behold.

CHAPTER 2

THE WINNER'S GAME

EVERYONE LIKES TO SUCCEED IN INVESTING. MILLIONS OF PEOPLE depend on investment success to assure their security in retirement, to provide for their children's education, or to enjoy better lives. Schools, hospitals, museums, and colleges depend on successful investing to fulfill their important missions. When investment professionals help investors achieve their realistic long-term objectives, investment management is a noble profession.

The accumulating evidence, however, compels the recognition that most investors are suffering serious shortfalls. The largest part of the problem is that investors make mistakes. But they are not alone. Investment professionals need to recognize that much of the real fault lies not with their clients but with themselves—the unhappy consequence of three major systemic errors. Fortunately, all professional investors can, and should, make changes to help ensure investing is, for both their client investors and themselves, truly a winner's game.

For all its amazing complexity, the field of investment management really has only two major parts. One is the *profession*: doing what is best for the returns for investment clients, and the other is the *business*: doing what is best for the profits of investment managers. As in other professions, such as law, medicine, architecture, and management consulting, there is a continuing struggle between the *values* of the profession and the *economics* of the business.

Investment firms must be successful at both to retain the trust of clients and to maintain a viable business—and in the long run, the latter depends on the former. Investment management differs from many other professions in one most unfortunate way: it is losing the struggle to put professional values and responsibilities first and business objectives second. To stop losing this struggle, investment firms need to emphasize investment counseling to help clients focus on the game that they can win *and* is worth winning. Fortunately, what is good for professional fulfillment can also be good for the investment firms' business—because delivering what clients need is always, in the long run, good business.

While the investment *profession*, like all learned professions, has many unusually difficult aspects that require great skill and is getting more complex almost daily, it too has just two major parts. One is the increasingly difficult task of *price discovery*—somehow combining imaginative research and astute portfolio management to achieve superior investment results by outsmarting the ever-more-numerous professional investors who now dominate the markets and collectively set the prices of securities. Always interesting, often fascinating, and sometimes exhilarating, the work of price discovery and competing to "beat the market," as we shall see, has been getting harder for many years and is now extraordinarily difficult. That's why most active investors are *not* beating the market; the market is beating them.

Difficulty is not always proportional to importance. (In medicine, simply washing hands has proven to be second only to penicillin in saving lives.) Fortunately, the most valuable part of what investment professionals can do is the least difficult: investment counseling, the second part.

Experienced professionals can help each client think through and determine the sensible investment program most likely to achieve his or her realistic long-term objectives within the client's own tolerance for various risks—such as variations in income, changes in market values, or constraints on liquidity. This can help each client stick with a sensible investment program, particularly when markets seem full of exciting "this time it's different" opportunities or fraught with disconcerting "it's gotten even worse" threats.[1] Success in staying on course is not simple or easy but is much easier, far more important, and has far more impact than success in active management. With the new tools available to investment professionals,[2] this is getting easier even as superior investing is getting steadily harder to achieve.

With remarkable irony, those devoting their careers to investment management have unintentionally created for themselves three problems. Two are errors of commission with increasingly serious consequences. The third is an even graver error, of omission.

The first error is to define the professional mission falsely to clients and prospective clients as "beating the market." Fifty years ago, those taking up that definition of mission had good prospects of success. But those years are long gone. In today's intensely competitive securities markets, few active managers outperform the market over the long term, most managers fall short, and in terms of magnitude, *under*performance substantially exceeds *out*performance. In addition, identifying the few managers who will be the future "winners" is notoriously difficult,[3] and the rate of subsequent failure among onetime "market leaders" is high.[4]

The grim reality of this first error of commission is that investment firms continue selling what most have not delivered and, in all likelihood, will not deliver: beat-the-market investment performance.

The stock market is not your grandfather's stock market anymore. Truly massive changes have transformed the markets and investment management so greatly that beating the market is no longer a realistic objective—as more and more investors are slowly recognizing.

Here are some of the changes that have compounded over 50 years to convert active investing into a loser's game:

- New York Stock Exchange trading volume is up more than one *thousand* times—from about 3 million shares a day to over 5 *billion*. Other major exchanges around the world have seen comparable changes in volume.
- The mix of investors has changed profoundly—from 90 percent of total NYSE listed trading done by individuals who averaged one trade every year or two to more than 98 percent done by institutions or computers operating in the market all day every day. And anyone with a long memory will tell you that today's institutional investors are far bigger, smarter, tougher, and faster than those of yore.
- Derivatives have surged in value traded from nil to larger than the "cash" market—and almost all derivatives trading is institutional.
- Over 120,000 analysts—up from zero 50 years ago—have earned Chartered Financial Analyst credentials, and an additional 200,000 are CFA candidates.
- Regulation Fair Disclosure, commonly known as Reg FD, has "commoditized" most investment information now coming from corporations. What was once the treasured secret sauce of traditional, research-based active investing is now by law just a commodity. Public companies must tell everybody everything they tell anyone—and tell it all at the same time via Twitter or another assured method.
- Algorithmic trading, computer models, and numerous inventive "quants" are powerful market participants.
- Globalization, hedge funds, and private equity funds have become major forces for change toward consistent fair value for all securities.

- Investment research reports from major securities firms produce an enormous volume of useful information that gets distributed instantly via the Internet to hundreds of thousands of expert analysts and portfolio managers around the world, working in fast-response decision-making organizations.
- More than 320,000 Bloomberg terminals spew all sorts of data, and virtually any desired analysis, 24 hours a day.
- The Internet and e-mail have created a technological revolution in global communications. Investors really are "all in this together," and almost everyone knows almost everything all the time.

As a result of these and many other changes, the stock markets—the world's largest and most active "prediction markets"—have become increasingly efficient. So it is more and more difficult to compete with all the smart, hardworking professionals, with all their information, computing power, and experience, who set those market prices. And it's much, much more difficult for any investor to beat the market—the consensus of experts—particularly after costs and fees.

Sadly, most descriptions of "performance" do not even mention the most critical aspect of investing: risk. So it is important to recall that the "losers" underperform the market one and one-half *times* as much as the "winners" outperform. Nor do the data adjust for taxes, particularly the high taxes on short-term gains that come with the now-normal 60 to 80 percent portfolio turnover.[5] Finally, performance for funds is usually reported as *time* weighted, not *value* weighted, so the reported data do not reflect the true investor experience. That can only be shown with the value-weighted record of how real investors have fared with their real money. It is not a pretty picture.

Nor is it comforting to see the details of how clients—both individuals and institutions—turn negative toward their investment managers after a few years of underperformance and switch to managers with a "hot" recent record, positioning themselves for another round of buy-high, sell-low dissatisfaction and obliterating roughly one-third of their funds' actual long-term returns. (Individuals who actively manage their own investments, notoriously, do even worse.)

Unfortunately, this costly behavior is encouraged by investment firms that, to increase sales, concentrate their advertising on a few funds clearly selected because of their stellar recent results—over carefully selected time periods that make good results look even better.[6] (Some fund managers have several hundred different funds, so they will always have at least some documented winners.) In hiring new managers, individual investors tend to rely on past performance even though studies of mutual funds show that for 9 out of 10 deciles of past performance, future performance is virtually random. (Only one decile's past results have predictive power: the worst, or 10th decile—apparently because high fees and chronic incompetence have a repetitively negative impact on investment results.)[7] The sad truth is that time and again investors, both institutional and individual, buy *after* the best results and sell out *after* the worst is over. This behavior is costly to investors.[8]

When they earn the trust and confidence of their clients, investment advisors can add far more to long-term returns than active managers can hope to produce.[9] Effective investment counseling takes time, and learning the complexities of markets, investing, and investors is hard work. But it can be done and done well, repeatedly. Successful advisors will help each client understand the risks of investing, set realistic investment objectives, be sensible about saving and spending, select the appropriate asset classes, allocate assets wisely, and—most important—not overreact to market highs or lows. Advisors can help their clients stay the course and maintain a long-term perspective by helping them understand what each type of investment can achieve over the long haul, anticipate market price fluctuations, understand predictably disconcerting market turbulence, and be confident that over the year investment results will reward their patience and fortitude.

The second error of commission is allowing the values of the investment *profession* to become dominated by the economics of the investment *business*. It is at least possible that the talented and competitive people attracted to investment management have, however unintentionally, gotten so caught up in the superb economic rewards of the investment business that they are not asking potentially disruptive questions about the real value of their best efforts—particularly when they know they are unusually capable and working terribly hard. Consider the two main ways the profitability of investment management has increased over the past 50 years:

- Assets managed, with only occasional short pauses, have risen tenfold—partly due to market prices and partly due to increasing contributions.
- Fees, as a percentage of assets, have multiplied more than five times.

The combination of these two forces has proven powerful. As a result of strongly increasing profitability in the investment management business, compensation for highly skilled individuals has increased nearly tenfold and enterprise values are way, way up.

As investment management organizations have gotten larger, it is not surprising that business managers have increasingly displaced investment professionals in senior leadership positions or that business disciplines have increasingly dominated the old professional priorities. Business disciplines focus the attention of those with strong career ambitions on boosting profits, which is best achieved by increased "asset gathering"—even though investment professionals know that expanding the assets managed usually works against investment performance. (When business dominates, it is *not* the friend of the investment profession.)

The third error—an error of omission—is particularly troubling: losing sight of the professional opportunity to focus on effective investment counseling.[10] Most investors are understandably not experts on contemporary investing. Many need help. All would appreciate having access to the intelligent thinking and judgment that many investment professionals are well positioned to provide. Investors need a realistic understanding of the long-term and intermediate prospects for different kinds of investments—risk and volatility first, rate of return second—so they will know what to expect and how to determine their strategic portfolios and investment policies.

Still more important, most investors need help in developing a balanced and objective understanding of themselves and their situation: their investment knowledge and skills; their tolerance for risk in assets, incomes, and liquidity; their realistic time horizon; their financial and psychological needs; their financial resources; their financial aspirations and obligations in both the short and the long run; and so forth. Investors need to know that the problem they most want to address and solve is not beating the market. It is dealing effectively with the combination of those other factors—particularly their own ability to stay the course—that creates their reality as investors.

Although all investors are the same in several ways, they are very different in many more ways. All investors are the same in that they have many choices and are free to choose, their choices matter, and they want to do well and avoid doing harm. At the same time, all investors differ in very many ways: assets, income, spending obligations and expectations, investment time horizons, investment skills, tolerance of risk and uncertainty, market experience, and financial responsibilities. With all these differences, most investors (both individuals and institutions) need help in developing a solid understanding of who they really are as investors, what investment program will work best for each of them—and how to hang in there when markets are most disconcerting.

Skiing provides a useful analogy. At Vail or Aspen, thousands of skiers are enjoying happy days, partly because the scenery is beautiful, partly because the snow is plentiful and the slopes are groomed, but primarily because each skier has chosen the well-marked trails best suited to his or her skills, strength, and interests. Some like gentle "bunny slopes," some like moderately challenging intermediate slopes, some are more advanced, and still others want to try out trails that are challenging even for fearless experts in their late teens with spring-steel legs. When each skier is on the trail that is right for her or him and skiing that trail at the pace that is right for her or him, everyone has a great day and all are winners.

Similarly, when investment advisors guide investors to investment programs that are right for their investing skills and experience, their financial situations, and their individual tolerance for risk and uncertainty, most investors can match these programs with their own investment skills and resources and regularly achieve their own realistic, long-term objectives. This is the important work of investment counseling. Developing the investment program that is right for each unique investor is the real secret of how to succeed as an investment advisor.

Notes

1. As kids familiar with the realities of sailing, we cheerfully terrified our landlubber cousins by going out on a windy day and deliberately tacking close to the wind to cause our small sailboat to heel far over, knowing that when the boat seemed

most certainly about to capsize, the "righting arm" of the keel was even more certain to prevent its tipping any farther.

2. For example, Financial Engines (https://advisors.financial engines.com) and MarketRiders (http://www.marketriders .com).

3. Even close observers are hard-pressed to isolate the impact of luck versus skill when trying to evaluate the performance records of specific investment managers.

4. Of the 20 leading investment managers serving U.S. pension funds 40 years ago, Greenwich Associates' annual research shows that only 1 is still in the top 20. In the United Kingdom, only 2 of the top 20 investment managers of 30 years ago continue to be leaders.

5. With institutional portfolios turning over, on average, 60 percent a year—with 60 to 90 different positions, frequent comparisons with their benchmarks, and little tolerance for long periods of underperformance—portfolio managers are understandably hard-pressed to keep up with the market, let alone get ahead of their numerous and skillful competitors.

6. Managers of institutional funds often—surely all too often—join in the deception by showing performance data to clients and prospects *gross* of fees rather than *net* of fees as do all mutual funds. For many years, CFA Institute has advocated reform to address this issue.

7. John C. Bogle, *Don't Count on It!* (Hoboken, NJ: John Wiley & Sons, 2011), 74.

8. Terrance Odean of the University of California, Berkeley, has produced the best available data.

9. Institutional investors may well ask, "How can this be? Didn't our consultants' presentation show that the managers they recommend usually outperform their benchmarks? So shouldn't their managers be earning *something* above the market even after fully adjusting for risk?" Unfortunately for those holding this hopeful view, the data usually shown by

most consultants are flawed. By simply removing two biases in the data as conventionally presented—backdating and survivor bias—the apparent record of managers monitored by consultants often shifts down from "better than the market" appearances to "below the market" realities. Even large and sophisticated institutions should know who is watching the watchmen.

10. This is surely indicated by the substantial use of investment consultants, a subindustry that has grown to fill the investment advisory vacuum left by active managers. Many consultants give remarkably generic investment advice at meetings that focus on the transactions of hiring and firing managers and all too often are staffed by individuals whose real priority is maintaining their books of business by keeping accounts comfortable.

CHAPTER 3

BEATING THE MARKET

THE ONLY WAY ACTIVE INVESTMENT MANAGERS CAN BEAT THE market, after adjusting for market risk, is to discover and exploit other active investors' mistakes. (Note that in a liquid, professional market, prices are set by those with the most confidence that they know more than the current consensus and who are willing to commit substantial money to back up their judgment.)

Of course, in theory, beating the market *can* be done, and it has been done by many investors *some* of the time. However, very few investors have been able to outsmart and outmaneuver other expert investors often enough and regularly enough to beat the market consistently over the long term, particularly after covering all the costs of "playing the game." Ironically, the reason so few investors do better than the market is *not* because they lack skill or diligence but rather because the markets are dominated by other investing experts, who are very capable, well informed, and working all the time.

In theory, active investment managers can try to succeed with one of, *or* a combination of, four investment approaches:

- Market timing
- Selecting specific stocks or groups of stocks
- Making timely changes in portfolio structure or strategy
- Developing and implementing a superior, long-term investment concept or philosophy

Even the most casual observer of markets and companies will be impressed by the splendid array of apparent—and enticing—opportunities to "do better than" merely settling for average. The major changes in price charts for the overall market, for major industry groups, *and* for individual stocks make it seem deceptively obvious that active investors *must* be able to do better. After all, we've seen with our own eyes that the real stars perform consistently better than average in such diverse fields as sports, theater, law, and medicine, so why not in investing? Why shouldn't quite a few investment managers be consistently above average? And why should it be all that hard to beat the market?

Let's take a careful look.

The most audacious way to increase potential returns is through market timing. The classic "market timer" moves the portfolio in and out of the market so that it is fully invested during rising markets and substantially out of the market when prices are falling badly. Another form of timing would shift an equity portfolio out of stock groups that are expected to underperform the market and into groups expected to outperform.

But remember: every time you decide to get into or out of the market, the investors you buy from or sell to are professionals. Of course, the pros are not *always* right, but how confident are you that you will be more right more often than they will be? What's more, market timers incur trading costs with each and every move. And unless you are managing a tax-sheltered retirement account, you will have to pay taxes every time you take a profit. Over and over, the benefits of market timing prove illusory. The costs are real—and keep adding up.

Investment history documents conclusively that the very first weeks of a market recovery produce a substantial proportion of all the gains that will eventually be experienced. Yet it is at the crucial market bottom that a market timer is most likely to be *out* of the market—and thereby missing the very best part of the recovery gains.

Market timing does not work because in today's highly competitive market no manager is much more astute or insightful or
has more or better information—on a repetitive basis—than all
those professional competitors. In addition, many of the stock
market gains occur in very brief periods and at times when investors are most likely to be captives of a conventional consensus.

In a bond portfolio, the market timer hopes to shift into long
maturities before falling interest rates drive up long-bond prices
and back into short maturities before rising interest rates drive
down long-bond prices. In a balanced portfolio, the market timer
strives to invest more heavily in stocks when they will produce
greater total returns than bonds, then shift back into bonds
when they will produce greater total returns than stocks, then
into short-term investments when they will produce greater total
returns than either bonds or stocks. Unfortunately, on average,
these moves don't work because the sellers are just as smart as
the buyers, and the buyers are just as smart as the sellers, and
both groups know the same facts at the same time. And the more
frequently these moves are tried, the more certainly they fail
to work.

Perhaps the best insight into the difficulties of market timing
came from one experienced professional's candid lament: "I've
seen lots of interesting approaches to market timing—and I have
tried most of them in my 40 years of investing. They may have
been great before my time, but not one of them worked for me.
Not one!"

Just as there are *old* pilots and there are *bold* pilots, but no old,
bold pilots, there are *no* investors who have achieved recurring
successes in market timing. The market does just as well, on
average, when the investor is *out* of the market as it does when
he or she is *in* it. Therefore, the investor loses money relative to a
simple buy-and-hold strategy by being out of the market part of
the time. Wise investors don't even *consider* trying to outguess or
outmaneuver the market by selling high and buying low.

One reason is particularly striking. Figure 3.1 shows what happens to long-term compounded returns when the *best* days are removed from a 36-year record of nearly 10,000 trading days. Taking out only the 10 best days—one-tenth of 1 percent of the long period examined—cuts the average rate of return by 19 percent (from 11.4 percent to 9.2 percent). Taking away the 20 *next* best days cuts returns by an additional 17 percent. Figure 3.2 shows a similar result when the best *year* or *years* are excluded from the calculation of the long-term averages.

Figure 3.1 How Missing a Few Days Would Hurt Returns

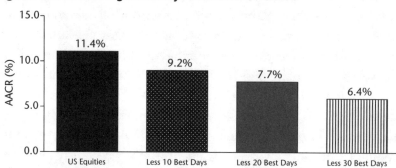

Source: Courtesy of Cambridge Associates (Period covered: January 1, 1980–April 30, 2016)

Figure 3.2 How Missing a Few Years Would Hurt Returns

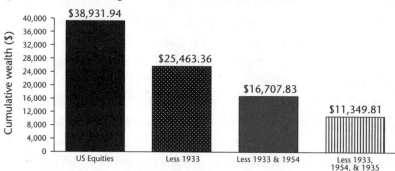

Source: Courtesy of Cambridge Associates (Period covered: January 1, 1980 – April 30, 2016)

Using the S&P 500 average returns, the story is told quickly and clearly: *All* the total returns on stocks in 20 years were achieved in the best 35 days—way less than 1 percent of the 5,000 trading days over two decades. (Imagine the "Walter Mitty" profits if we could simply know which days! Alas, we cannot and never will.) What we now know is both simple and valuable: If you missed those few and fabulous best days, you missed *all* the returns over two long decades.

Removing just the five best *days* out of 72 *years* of investing would reduce cumulative compound returns, without dividend investments, by nearly 50 percent.[1] (Seductively, for those willing to be seduced, sidestepping the 90 *worst* trading days would have resulted in a 10-year gain of $42.78.) If an investor missed just the 10 best days over the past 112 years—that's 10 days out of 49,910 days—he or she would have missed two-thirds of the total gains.[2]

One of the ways investors hurt themselves over the long run is to get frightened out of the market when the market has been awful and as a result miss the surprisingly important "best" days, when the market turns. The lesson is clear: You have to be there when lightning strikes. That's why market timing is a truly wicked idea. Don't try it—ever.

The second theoretical way to increase returns is through tactical stock selection, or "stock picking." Professional investors devote extraordinary skill, time, and effort to this work. Stock valuation dominates the research efforts of investing institutions and the research services of stockbrokers all over the world.

Through financial analysis and field research on a company's competitors and suppliers, as well as management interviews, professional investors strive to attain an understanding of the investment value of a security or group of securities that is better than the market consensus. When investment managers find significant differences between the market price and the value of a security as they appraise it, they can buy or sell in an effort to capture for their clients' portfolios the differential between market price and true investment value. This attempt to get ahead of the competition at price discovery was at least possible before

Reg FD and the commoditization of information that, with all the other changes, have made stock markets so hard to beat.

Unfortunately, security analysis taken as a whole does not appear to be a profitable activity. The stocks investment managers sell after doing fundamental research, and the stocks they don't buy, typically do about as well relative to the overall market as the stocks they do buy. Because they are so large, so well informed, and so active, institutional investors collectively set the prices. That's why the only way to beat the market is to beat the professionals who, as a group, *are* the market.

The problem is *not* that investment research is not done well. The problem is that research is done so very well by so many. Research analysts at major brokerage firms share their information and evaluations almost instantly through global networks with thousands of professional investors who strive to act quickly in anticipation of how others will soon act. As a result, it is very hard to gain and sustain a repetitive useful advantage over all the other investors on stock selection or price discovery. As experts sell to one another and buy from one another, academics say they are making the market pricing mechanism "efficient."

Strategic decisions, the third way to try to increase returns in both stock and bond portfolios, involve making major commitments that affect the overall structure of the portfolio. These decisions are made to exploit insights into major industry groups, changes in the economy and interest rates, or anticipated shifts in the valuation of major types of stocks, such as "emerging growth" stocks or "value" stocks.

Full of interesting potential—*if* moving the portfolio to the right place at the right time—this approach to investing challenges the investor to discover a new "edge" or way to invest as markets shift, to become proficient at each new way, and then to abandon that new way for a *new* new way when other investors have recognized the prior insight (or the insight was a misperception *or* was already "in the price" and accepted by the consensus of experts). In theory, of course, this *can* be done, but *will* it be done? Sure, it will be done occasionally, but by which managers? And how often?

The long-term record is *not* encouraging. The record of individual investors identifying in advance which managers will succeed is downright discouraging. For example, in the late 1990s, those investors who were most committed to technology enjoyed a wonderful romp—until the sharp market correction in 2000. (The market giveth, and the market taketh away.) Then, in the early part of the first decade of the twenty-first century, financial stocks did well—until they led the 2008–2009 market collapse.

In the early 1970s, portfolio managers who invested heavily in large capitalization growth stocks—the "Nifty 50"—experienced exceptionally favorable results as the notorious "two tier" market continued to develop. (Growth stocks had much higher price/earnings ratios than industrial stocks, thus dividing the market into two tiers.) But by the late 1970s, owning the same securities produced exceptionally negative results: as anticipated earnings failed to materialize, investors became disenchanted with the "hold forever" concept and dumped their holdings. The same thing happened with oil stocks in the '80s *and* in 2016, to major pharmaceuticals in the '90s, and to commodities in the first decade of the twenty-first century. All too often, at the peak, the confident consensus is, "This time it's different!" The same up, up, up, *down* phenomenon has been repeated many times.

Another possible way to increase returns is for an individual portfolio manager or an entire investment management organization to develop a profound and valid insight into the forces that will drive superior long-term investment results in a particular sector of the market or a particular group of companies or industries and then systematically exploit that investment insight or concept through cycle after cycle in the business economy and in the stock market.

An investment organization that is committed, for example, to growth-stock investing will concentrate on evaluating new technologies, understanding the management skills required to lead a rapidly growing business, and analyzing the financial requirements for investing in new markets and new products to sustain growth. This organization will strive to learn from experience—sometimes painful experience—how to discriminate between ersatz growth stocks that fizzle out and true growth companies that will achieve serial successes over many years.

Other fund managers take the view that, among the many large corporations in mature and often cyclical industries, there are always some that have considerably greater investment value than most investors recognize. Such investment organizations strive to develop expertise in separating the wheat from the chaff, avoiding the low-priced stocks that really *ought* to be low priced. These managers believe that with astute research they can isolate superior long-term values and, by buying good value at depressed prices, achieve superior returns for their clients with relatively low risk.

The important test of an investment concept or philosophy is the manager's ability to adhere to it persistently for valid, long-term reasons even when the short-term results are disagreeable. The great advantage of a major conceptual or philosophical approach is that the investment firm can organize itself to do its own particular kind of investing all the time, avoid the noise and confusion of distracting alternatives, attract investment analysts and managers interested in and skilled at the particular type of investing, and—through continuous practice, self-critique, and study—develop real mastery. The great disadvantage is that if the chosen kind of investing becomes obsolete, overpriced, or out of touch with the changing market, a focused specialist organization is unlikely to detect the need for change until it has become too late—both for its clients and for itself.

What is remarkable about profound investment concepts is how few have been discovered that have lasted for long—most likely because the hallmark of a free capital market is that few if any opportunities to establish a proprietary long-term competitive conceptual advantage can be found and maintained for long.

The market for good investment ideas is among the best in the world; word gets around very quickly.

All forms of active investing have one fundamental characteristic in common: *they depend on the errors of others.* Whether by omission or commission, the only way a profit opportunity can be available to an active investor is for the consensus of other professional investors to be *wrong.* Although this sort of collective error does occur, we must ask how often these errors are made and how often any particular manager will avoid making similar errors at the same time and instead have the wisdom, skill, and courage to take action opposed to the consensus. One way to increase success in lifelong investing is to reduce mistakes. (Ask any golfer, tennis player, or driving instructor how beneficial reducing errors can be.)

With so many competitors simultaneously seeking superior insight into the value/price relationship of individual stocks or industry groups, and with so much information so widely and rapidly communicated throughout the investment community, the chances of discovering and exploiting profitable insights into individual stocks or groups of stocks—opportunities left behind by the errors and inattention of other investors—are certainly not richly promising.

Many investors make the mistake of trying too hard, striving to get more from their investments than those investments can produce—typically by borrowing heavily on margin to increase leverage—and thus courting serious disappointment. All too often, trying too hard is eventually expensive because taking too much risk *is* too much risk.

An opposite mistake investors make is not trying hard enough, usually by being too defensive and letting short-term anxieties dominate long-term thinking and long-term behavior. Over the long run, it has been costly to maintain even a modest cash reserve within an equity portfolio.

With so many apparent "opportunities" to do better than the market, it can be difficult for inexperienced investors to accept how hard it is in real life to do better than the market over the long haul. Even the most talented investment managers must wonder how they can expect their hardworking and determined competitors to provide—through incompetence, error, or inattention—sufficiently attractive opportunities to buy or sell on such a regular basis that they can repeatedly beat the market by beating them.

Even after recognizing that market timing does not work, outside observers often wonder about the stock market's major moves. If the market is so darned efficient, why does it go up and down so much? Surely, the true value does not go up so much or down so much or, in either case, so swiftly!

Of course not. But *perceptions* of future value always anticipate estimates—estimates of other investors' estimates of still other investors' estimates of other investors' estimates. And the best indicators of change in investors' estimates of estimates, etc. are changes in pricing. The market's pricing mechanism is neither stable nor consistent. So just as the apocryphal "butterfly of chaos" can change weather and cause violent storms, the market can behave "irrationally." Why? because diligent, rational people—ready to react quickly to any change in perceptions of others' perceptions—try to anticipate a market that reacts to all sorts of bits and pieces of new information (or, of course, misinformation). That's why economists laugh about the stock market anticipating nine of the last three recessions! But if all that "noise" in stock pricing were *not* rational, wouldn't someone have figured out by now how to profit from those collective errors?

To see the reality through an analogy, imagine yourself at an antique fair with dozens of open booths. When you arrive, hoping to find some lovely things for your home, you are given one of four scenarios. In the first, you will have two hours—alone—to look over the merchandise and make your selections.

In the second, you will be joined by two dozen other "special guest" expert shoppers for the same two hours.

In the third, you will be admitted to do your shopping for two days along with 1,000 other special ticket holders shortly *after* the two dozen experienced special guests have spent two hours making *their* selections.

In the final scenario, you will be one of 50,000 shoppers admitted—on the third day of the fair. In this last scenario, you *may* find a few objects you like at prices you think are reasonable, but you know you won't discover any antiques that are seriously mispriced bargains.

Now make a few *more* changes: All the shoppers are not only buyers, they are also sellers, each bringing and hoping to sell antiques they recently purchased at other fairs, and all are looking for ways to upgrade their collections. In addition, the prices of all transactions—and all past transactions—are known to all the market participants, who all studied antiques at the same famous schools and all have ready access to the same curators' reports from well-regarded museums.

This simple exercise reminds us that open markets with many expert and well-informed participants will do well at their primary function: price discovery. The problem is not that active investment managers are not skillful, but rather that collectively they have been becoming more skillful for many years *and* are coming to market in greater and greater numbers. So while a purist might claim that the major stock markets of the world are not perfect at matching price to value at every moment in time, most prices are too close to value—or will quickly move there—for any investor to profit regularly from the errors of others by enough to cover the fees and costs of making the effort.

So, while the market is not *perfectly* efficient, it's no longer worth the real costs of trying to beat it. That's why more and more investors are coming to agree that if you cannot beat 'em, you can join 'em by indexing, particularly for the Big Four reasons: (1) The stock markets have changed extraordinarily over the past 50 years; (2) indexing outperforms active investing; (3) index funds are low cost; and (4) indexing investment *operations* enable investors to focus their time and attention on the *policy* decisions that are so important for long-term investment success.

In the movie *Full Metal Jacket*, two crusty drill sergeants are watching their basic training class jogging in close-order drill to their graduation ceremony, shouting military calls like "Airborne! All the way!" One drill instructor says, "Sarge, what do you see when you look at those boys?" After the classic expectoration, the other replies, "What do I see? I'll tell ya. About 10 percent of those boys are honest to God *soldiers*!" Pause. "The rest . . . are just . . . targets!" That's just a scene from a war flick, but it has real-life meaning for every individual investor to ponder.

Here's a way to turn on the lights. Let's assume that you are so skilled and so well informed that you are in fact in the top 20 percent of all individual investors. Bravo! Take a bow—but then, watch out! Here's why. Even if you are a well-*above*-average individual investor compared with other individuals, you are almost certain to be making *below*-average trades in markets now dominated by the trading experts, who make millions of highly skilled trades each year—and more trades each *day*—than you and I would make in a lifetime. It's in the numbers.

The first step into reality is to recognize that the key to market success is *not* your skill and knowledge as an investor compared with other individual investors, but the skill and knowledge with which *each* specific investment *transaction* is made. So if 90 percent of the pros trade with more skill and knowledge than you have—which is, alas, quite likely—your transactions will, on average, be buried deep in the bottom quartile of all transactions.

In a paper titled "Why *Do* Investors Trade Too Much?," Terrance Odean, finance professor at the University of California, Berkeley, looked at nearly 100,000 stock trades made over 15 years by retail investors at a major discount brokerage firm. He found that, on average, the stocks these investors bought underperformed the market by 2.7 percentage points over the following year, while the stocks they sold outperformed the market by 0.5 point in the following year. Similarly, a paper published by Brookings Institution economists Josef Lakonishok, Andrei Shleifer, and Robert Vishny showed that the stock trades made by professional fund managers subtracted 0.78 percent from the returns they would have earned by keeping their portfolios constant. Finally, the Plexus Consulting Group, a firm that researches the costs of trading for professional money managers, studied more than 80,000 trades by 19 investment firms and found that while the typical purchase of a stock added 0.67 percent to a fund's short-term return, the typical sale subtracted 1.8 percent.

Las Vegas, Macao, and Monaco are busy every day, so we know not everyone is entirely rational. If you, like Walter Mitty, still fantasize that you can and will beat the pros, you'll need both good luck *and* our prayers.

Meanwhile, experienced investors understand four powerful truths about investing, and wise investors will govern their investing by adhering to them:

1. The dominating reality of investing is that the most important decision is your chosen long-term mix of assets: how much in stocks, real estate, bonds, or cash.
2. That asset mix should be determined partly by your real purpose for the money, partly by when the money will be used, and partly by your ability to stay the course.
3. Diversify within each asset class and among asset classes. Bad things do happen—usually as surprises.
4. Be patient and persistent. Good things come in spurts—usually when least expected—and fidgety investors fare badly. "Plan your play and play your plan," say the great coaches, and that takes you back to number 1.

Curiously, most investors, who all say they are trying to get better performance, do themselves and their portfolios real harm by going against one or all of these truths. They do not concentrate time and attention on determining their optimal balance among asset classes. Their portfolio structure is not tailored to the time when the money will be spent. They diversify too little, so they take more risk than they realize—until too late: the risk becomes reality. And they have too little long-term patience and persistence to stay the course. In addition, they pay higher fees, incur the costs of change, and pay more taxes.

They spend hours of time and lots of emotional energy and accumulate "loss leaks" that drain away the results they could have had from their investments if they had only taken the time and care to understand their own investment realities, develop the sensible long-term program most likely to achieve their real goals, and then stay the course with that program.

The importance of being realistic about investment markets gets greater as the markets are increasingly dominated by large, fast-acting, well-informed professionals armed with major advantages. And over the past 20 years, more than four out of five of the pros got beaten by the market averages—as we would see *if* accurate and complete records were published. For individuals, the grim reality is surely far worse.

Notes

1. On Wall Street, the coming of summer is marked with stories about the "summer rally," the fall is heralded by laments about October being the worst month for stocks (statistically, September has been worse), and the turn of the year is celebrated with "the January effect," which doesn't always arrive. Mark Twain's comments about the stock market may have said it best: "October. This is one of the peculiarly dangerous

months to speculate in stocks. The others are July, January, September, April, November, May, March, June, December, August, and February" (*Pudd'nhead Wilson*, 1894).

2. Jason Zweig was reporting in the *Wall Street Journal* on research by Javier Estrada.

CHAPTER 4

MR. MARKET AND
MR. VALUE

THE STOCK MARKET IS FASCINATING *AND* QUITE DECEPTIVE—IN the short run. Over the very long run, the market can be almost boringly reliable and predictable.

Understanding the personalities of two very different characters is vital to a realistic understanding of the stock market. These very different characters are "Mr. Market" and "Mr. Value."

Mr. Market gets all the attention because he's so interesting, while poor old Mr. Value goes about his important work almost totally ignored by investors. It's not fair. Mr. Value does all the work, while Mr. Market has all the fun and causes all the trouble.

Introduced by Benjamin Graham in his classic book *The Intelligent Investor*,[1] Mr. Market occasionally lets his enthusiasms or his fears run wild. Emotionally unstable, Mr. Market sometimes feels euphoric and sees only the favorable factors affecting a business; at other times he feels so depressed that he can see nothing but trouble ahead. This most accommodating fellow stands ready, day after day, to buy if we want to sell or to sell if we want to buy. Totally unreliable and quite unpredictable, Mr. Market tries again and again to get us to do something, anything, but at least something. For him, the more activity, the better. To provoke us to action, he keeps changing his prices—sometimes quite rapidly.

Mr. Market is a mischievous but captivating fellow who persistently teases investors with gimmicks and tricks such as surprising earnings reports, startling dividend announcements, sudden surges of inflation, inspiring presidential pronouncements, grim news of commodities prices and ugly bankruptcies, exciting revelations of amazing new technologies, and even serious threats of war. These events come from his big bag of tricks when they are least expected.

Just as magicians use clever deceptions to divert our attention, Mr. Market's very short-term distractions can trick us and confuse our thinking about investments. Mr. Market dances before us without a care in the world. And why not? He has no responsibilities at all. As an economic gigolo, he has only one objective: to be "attractive."

Meanwhile, Mr. Value, a remarkably stolid and consistent fellow, never shows—and seldom stimulates—any emotion. He lives in the cold, hard real world, where there is nary a thought about perceptions or feelings. He works all day and all night inventing, making, and distributing goods and services. His job is to grind it out on the shop floor, at the warehouse, and in the retail store—day after day, doing the *real* work of the economy. His role may not be emotionally exciting, but it sure is important.

Mr. Value always prevails in the long run. Eventually, Mr. Market's antics, like sand castles on the beach, come to naught. In the real world of business, goods and services are produced and distributed in much the same way and in much the same volume when Mr. Market is up as they are when he's down. Long-term investors need to avoid being shaken or distracted by Mr. Market from their sound policies for achieving favorable long-term results. (Similarly, wise parents of teenagers avoid hearing—or remembering—too much of what their children say in moments of stress.)

The daily weather is comparably different from the climate. Weather is about the short run. Climate is about the long run, and that makes all the difference. In choosing a climate in which to build a home, we would not be deflected by last week's weather. Similarly, in choosing a long-term investment program, we don't want to be deflected by temporary market conditions.

Investors should ignore that rascal Mr. Market and his constant jumping around. The daily changes in the market are no more important to a long-term investor than the daily weather is to a climatologist or to a family deciding where to make their permanent home. Investors who wisely ignore the deceptive tricks of Mr. Market and pay little or no attention to current price changes will look instead at their *real* investments in *real* companies—and to their growing earnings and dividends—and will concentrate on real results over the long term.

Because Mr. Market always uses surprising short-term events to grab our attention, spark our emotions, and trick us, experienced investors study long-term stock market history to understand what really matters. Similarly, airline pilots spend hours and hours in flight simulators, "flying" through simulated storms and other unusual crises so they are accustomed to all sorts of otherwise stressful circumstances and are well prepared to remain calm and rational when faced with those situations in real life. The more you study market history, the better; the more you know about how securities markets *have* behaved in the past, the more you'll understand their true nature and how they probably *will* behave in the future.

Such an understanding enables us to live rationally with markets that would otherwise seem wholly irrational. At least, we would not so often get shaken loose from our long-term thinking by the short-term tricks and deceptions of Mr. Market's gyrations. Knowing history and understanding its lessons can insulate us from being surprised. Just as a teenage driver is genuinely amazed by his or her all-too-predictable accidents—"Dad, the guy came out of *nowhere!*"—investors can be surprised by adverse performance caused by "anomalies" and "six sigma events." Actually, those surprises are all within the market's normal bell-curve distribution of experiences. For the serious student of markets, they are not truly surprises: most are really almost actuarial *expectations*, and long-term investors should not overreact.

The same goes for pilots. In *The Right Stuff*, Tom Wolfe tells how "unique events" keep causing serious "inexplicable" accidents among superb test pilots. The young pilots never catch on to the reality that these very unusual events are, sadly, an integral part of the dangers inherent in their striving to achieve superior performance by flying far outside their comfort zones to frontiers no other pilot has attempted.

Of course, most professional investment managers would have good performance—comfortably better than the market averages—*if* they could eliminate a few "disappointing" investments or a few "difficult" periods in the market. (And most teenagers would have fine driving records if they could expunge a few "surprises.") However, the grim reality of life is that most investment managers and most teenage drivers are almost certain to experience anomalous events. In investing, these events occur when an unusual or unanticipated event—one that the manager understandably sees as quite unexpected and almost certain never to recur in exactly the same way—suddenly wipes out what otherwise would have been superior investment performance.

And the long term in investing is inevitably dominated by regression to the mean. That's why unusually high stock prices—as much as you may enjoy them—are not really good for you. Eventually, you'll have to give back every single increment of return you get that's above the long-term central trend.

Investing is *not* entertainment—it's a sober responsibility—and investing is not supposed to be fun or "interesting." It's a continuous process, like refining petroleum or manufacturing cookies, chemicals, or integrated circuits. If anything in the process is "interesting," it's almost surely *wrong*. That's why benign neglect is, for most investors, the secret to long-term success.

The biggest challenge in the stock market is not Mr. Market or Mr. Value. The biggest challenge is neither visible nor measurable; it is hidden in the emotional incapacities of each of us as investors. Investing, like parenting teenagers, benefits from calm, patient persistence; a long-term perspective; and constancy to purpose. The biggest risk in investing is almost always the short-term behavior of the investor. That's why "know thyself" is the cardinal rule for all investors. The hardest work in investing is not intellectual; it's emotional.

Being rational in an apparently irrational, hyperactive "anticipations of anticipations of anticipations" short-term environment is not easy, particularly with Mr. Market always trying to trick you into making changes. That's why the hardest work is not figuring out the optimal investment policy; it's sustaining a long-term focus—particularly at market highs or market lows—and staying committed to *your* optimal investment policy.

Note

1. Benjamin Graham, *The Intelligent Investor* (New York: Harper Collins, 1949).

CHAPTER 5

THE INVESTOR'S DREAM TEAM

THE LARGEST PART OF ANY PORTFOLIO'S TOTAL LONG-TERM return will come from the simplest investment decision— and by far the easiest to implement: buying the market by investing in index funds. If, like most investors, your instinct is to say, "Oh no! I don't want to settle for average. I want to beat the market!"[1] others may think quietly to themselves, "Alas, here's another Walter Mitty fantasizing that he'll beat the pros." Even so, let's offer you the help you'll need: your investor's dream team.

If you could have anyone—and everyone—you ever wanted as colleague-investors working with you all day every day, which great investors would you include on your investor's dream team?

Warren Buffett? Done deal. He and his partner, Charlie Munger, are on your team. David Swensen? Jack Meyer? Jane Mendillo? Paula Volent? Seth Alexander? They are all yours— plus all the analysts and fund managers at Fidelity and all the professionals at Capital Group. George Soros, David Einhorn, Steve Mandel, and Abby Joseph Cohen? Okay! They are on your side, too—and so are all the best hedge fund managers across the country.

Don't stop there. You can also have all the best analysts on Wall Street—250 at Merrill Lynch, 250 at Goldman Sachs, and 250 at Morgan Stanley—plus nearly equal numbers at Credit Suisse, UBS, and Deutsche Bank, and all the "boutique" broker analysts specializing in technology or emerging markets. You can have all the best portfolio managers worldwide and all the analysts who work for them on your dream team.

In fact, you can have all the best professionals working for you all the time. All you have to do is agree to accept all their best thinking without asking questions. (Most of us do the same sort of thing every time we fly: We know that our pilots are highly trained, experienced, and committed to safety, so we relax in our seats and leave the flying to the experts.)

To get the combined expertise of all these top professionals, all you have to do is index—because an index fund replicates the market, and today's professional-dominated stock market reflects the accumulated expertise of all those diligent experts making their best current judgments on pricing all the time. And as they learn more, they will quickly update their judgments, which means that you will always have the most up-to-date expert consensus when you index. Realistically, the stock market is the world's largest "prediction market," with many independent experts making their best predictions and putting up real money and their professional reputations to back their respective estimates.

When you index, not only do you get the advantages of having the investor's dream team working for you, you also automatically get other important benefits. Peace of mind is one. Most individual investors have to endure regret about their specific past mistakes—and worry about potential future regret. Indexing makes both unnecessary. And for those who go with the investor's dream team and index, there are several more powerful competitive advantages: lower fees, lower taxes, and lower "operating" expenses. These persistent costs of active investing mount up unrelentingly and do as much harm to investment portfolios as termites do to homes. Avoiding them by investing in index funds will make you a winner—beating over 80 percent of all other investors over the long haul, and that's before taxes.

While increasingly appreciated, particularly among experienced investors, accepting the consensus of the expert is not always popular. The pejoratives range from "just settling for average" to "un-American." The worst pejorative is the very name often used: passive. Try it: This is my husband; he's passive. I'll vote for X as president because she's passive.

Hopelessly unpopular with active investment managers—and with many hopeful investors—the "market portfolio," or index fund, is actually the result of all the hard work being done every day by the investor's dream team. Index investing is seldom given anything like the respect it deserves. But it will, over time, achieve better results than most mutual funds—and far better results than most individual investors.

Considering all the time, cost, and effort devoted to trying to achieve better-than-market results, the index fund certainly produces a lot of value for very little cost. This dull, workhorse portfolio may appear mindless, but it is in fact based on an extensive body of research on markets and investments that is well worth examining and can be briefly summarized as follows.

The securities markets are open, free, and competitive markets in which large numbers of well-informed and price-sensitive professional investors compete skillfully, vigorously, and continuously as both buyers and sellers. Nonexperts can easily retain the services of experts. Prices are quoted widely and promptly. Effective prohibitions against market manipulation are well established. And arbitrageurs, traders, hedge funds, private equity funds, market technicians, acquisitive corporations, and longer-term research-based investors continuously seek to find and profit from any market imperfections. Because competing investors are well-informed buyers and sellers—particularly when they are considered in the aggregate—it is unlikely that any one investment manager can regularly obtain profit increments for a large, diversified portfolio through fundamental research, because too many other equally dedicated professionals will also be using the best research they can obtain to make their appraisals of whether and when to sell or buy.

Such a market is considered "efficient"—not perfect, but sufficiently efficient that wise investors will recognize that they cannot expect to exploit inefficiencies regularly. The more numerous the skillful competitors, the less likely that any one of them can achieve consistently superior results. (Significantly, the number of well-educated, highly motivated people going into professional investing worldwide has been phenomenal.) In an efficient market, changes in prices follow the pattern described as a "random walk," which means that even close observers of the market will not be able to find patterns in changing securities prices with which to predict future price changes on which they might make profits.

In a perfectly efficient market, prices not only reflect any information that can be inferred from the historical sequence of prices, but they also incorporate all that is knowable about the companies whose stocks are being traded. (While there is some evidence that quarterly earnings reports are not immediately and completely discounted in securities prices, the apparent opportunities to be exploited are so limited in magnitude or duration that managers of large portfolios are not able to make effective use of this kind of information anyway.)

An efficient market does not mean that stocks will always sell at the "right" price. As everyone knows, markets fluctuate and, as in October 1987 or October–November 2008, "fluctuation" can be quite violent when fed by collective mistakes such as the exuberant dot-com and subprime mortgage markets. Note that investors can be quite wrong in their collective judgments on the overall market—overly optimistic or overly pessimistic, which will show up later in overall market corrections—and still be highly "efficient" at incorporating into relative market prices any available fundamental information about individual securities.

So the beginning of wisdom is understanding that few if any major investment organizations will outperform the market over long periods and that it is very difficult to estimate in advance which managers will outperform. The next step is to decide whether—even if it might be won—this loser's game is worth playing, particularly when indexing provides investment managers and their clients with an easy alternative. Indexers do not have to play the more complex games of equity investing—changing portfolio strategy, stock selection, and so forth—unless they want to. The freedom to invest at any time in an index fund is a marvelous freedom of choice because superior knowledge and skill are not consistent attributes of even the best investors. Given the intensity and skill of the competition, superior knowledge is exceedingly rare.

The option of using an index fund enables all investors to keep pace with the market virtually without effort. It allows us to play "active investing" and select any part of the wide investment spectrum for deliberate actions at any time for as long or as brief a period as we wish—but only when and where we really want to do it. This freedom not to play carries the reciprocal responsibility to invest away from index funds only when the incremental reward fully justifies the incremental risk.

Our most successful investor, Warren Buffett, recommends that investors consider indexing: "Let me add a few thoughts about your own investments. Most investors, both institutional and individual, will find that the best way to own common stocks is through an index fund that charges minimal fees. Those following this path are sure to beat the net results (after fees and expenses) delivered by the great majority of investment professionals."[2]

As every debater, negotiator, and litigator knows, the most important part of developing a convincing argument is to analyze the opponent's argument. So let's examine the pros and cons of the various arguments that advocates of active management make in opposition to index investing:

Table 5.1 Indexing: Assertions Versus Reality

"Active" Assertion	Realistic Response
Tracking error can be a problem for index funds in "small cap" stocks or emerging markets.	Yes, of course, because there are so many stocks to choose from and an index fund will construct its portfolio using a sample. So there will be imperfections. But the tracking error of index funds is far, far smaller than the tracking errors of active managers.
Index funds get stuck with overpriced large cap stocks, like GE in 2000.	True. And index funds also got stuck with those same stocks when they went from cheap to fairly priced to high priced.
Settling for "average" is not how America became the world's strongest economy and individual Americans achieved success. Passive investing, aimed at average, is un-American.	Stirring words, until the hard facts of history are examined. Matching the market average turns out to be the *winning* strategy because the "average" fund or institution and the "average" individual investor over and over again fall short of the market. So matching the market means doing *better* than the average investor—and over time, much better.
Active managers can "go defensive" when market prices are too high or economic uncertainties prevail. This can give active managers an advantage over passive indexing.	Some do, but some don't. Only a minority of active managers go defensive at exactly the right time. (Remember, a stopped clock is right twice a day.) Over the long term, market timers "go defensive" in almost random patterns that offset one another and, as a group, significantly reduce their clients' long-term returns.
Active management must work, or active managers would go out of existence.	Perceptions of potentials prevail. Casinos all over the world are jammed with players who, on average, are continuous losers—but keep returning. Active managers do believe they can beat the market—or they say they do. Even more important, so do their clients.
After fees, index funds underperform the markets they replicate.	Sure, but only by very little. Index funds charge as little as 0.10% and make back part of that small amount via securities lending. So for the very small net fee, investors get extensive diversification, convenience, and confidence. Far more important is this stunning finding from Morningstar: While the research firm's ubiquitous "star" ratings on past performance have little or no value in predicting future performance, low-fee funds in every category outperform other funds.

Several strong reasons for indexing are never mentioned by the advocates of active investment:

- Taxes. Index funds incur far less in tax liabilities because they have much lower turnover than actively managed funds—roughly 5 to 10 percent versus 60 to 80 percent or more—and report zero short-term profits, which, of course, are what incurs higher tax rates.
- High fees are a significant and unrelenting drain on an active manager's results. As Ben Franklin wisely said, "A penny saved is a penny earned."
- Costs. Trading costs are much lower for index funds than for active managers.
- Peace of mind. While all investors will experience the market's ups and downs, investors in index funds have no concerns about their manager's style changing or being "off" the market or their manager being acquired or, as so often happens to successful managers, being overloaded with money to invest.

Another way to examine the choice between indexing and active management is to flip the usual sequence and propose that an experienced indexer switch to active investing. The argument for changing to active might go like this: "Active investing gives investors the chance to do better than the market. In order to have that chance, however, a few problems must be accepted. Fees are more than 10 times higher. Over the longer term, 80 percent of active managers fall short of their self-selected benchmarks, and those that underperform do significantly worse than the "winners" do better. There is no known way to identify superior managers. Deteriorating managers—and there are many over the long term—are hard to identify before serious problems become evident in repeated performance shortfalls. And as an investor, you are always worried that your active manager will get into trouble."

Investors unable to devote the significant resources necessary to identify active managers who could outperform should take little or no risk with active managers. Instead, they should focus on developing an appropriate asset allocation and embrace index investing in each asset class to minimize fees. For most investors, the major benefit of indexing is that it silences Mr. Market and enables the investor to concentrate on the far more important macro decision of choosing the long-term investment program and asset mix with the best prospects of reaching each investor's own objectives.

Central to each investor's optimal investment strategy is determining the level of market risk to take. There is an optimal level of market risk specific to each investor. It is the level of market risk that is appropriate to the length of time that the investments will stay invested, and the market volatility the particular investor can live with to confidently stay the course. Sounds simple—and it is "simple"—but it's certainly not easy, particularly when Mr. Market is pushing all your buttons and tension is high.

Broadly, there are two major categories of risk in investing. One is investment risk; the other is investor risk. The first gets all the attention, but the second should be our focus because, while we can do very little about investment risk, every investor can make a major difference with a moderate effort on investor risk. The market is what it is. Mr. Market does what he does. As with the weather, we can choose an agreeable climate, but we must learn to accept the day-to-day changes as they come.

A small-boat sailor can do little to change the wind or tide but can do a lot by selecting the right course, keeping sails well trimmed, knowing what he and his boat can do in heavy weather, and watching the skies to avoid serious storms. Similarly, the investor can work with the markets to achieve her realistic objectives, but she must not take on more risk of heavy weather or possible market movements beyond her capacity to sustain commitments until the market storms have passed.

Active investors can do better, and some will do better some of the time. But if certain mutual fund managers had been doing significantly better for several years—particularly after taxes, fees, expenses, and errors—don't you suppose that, with everyone looking, we'd all know which funds they managed? And wouldn't we all want them to manage our money? And wouldn't we—all meaning to do the right thing—flood those funds with so much money that they would be overloaded? Of course we would.

That's why investors will be wise to devote attention to understanding the real advantages offered by the total market index fund—the product of all the skill and work being done every day by the investor's dream team.

Accepting reality is not always easy. And when it goes against someone's economic interests or obliges giving up a long-held set of beliefs—particularly when many others apparently hold on to those same beliefs—accepting reality can be very difficult. This is one of the best explanations of why so many active investment managers continue to resist indexing—even those who index some or all of their own investments.

While Darwinian evolution enjoys extensive scientific confirmation, over 40 percent of Americans still profess belief in creationism. And a similar percent still doubt global warming. Although serious students of reality may find it hard to understand why so many resist indexing and exchange-traded funds (ETFs) or somehow believe in creationism or do not yet believe in climate change, we should not be entirely surprised. Rejecting or even challenging a line of work is very difficult for those whose incomes—particularly large incomes—depend on its continuation.

As Thomas Kuhn explained in his classic *The Structure of Scientific Revolutions*, change is hard to accept for those who have built their careers developing all the follow-on particulars of a theory based on certain basic assumptions. To change from old assumptions and beliefs to a new set of assumptions is hard when we have a lot to lose in stature and income.

So it was with the skeptics in Washington, DC, who seized on major snowfalls as "proof" against global warming without checking to see if the data might actually confirm rather than deny global warming. (The snow was in fact strong confirmation of climate change.) As biologists probe ever more deeply into the way life really works, Darwinian evolution gets more and more confirmation. And so it is with indexing and ETFs.

Study after study adds to the accumulation of evidence that— with rare exceptions and only very rare exceptions that could have been discovered in advance—active management costs more than it produces in value added. No systematic studies support an alternate view. So what can we sensibly expect of the way people—many with strong economic, social, or emotional interests in continuing to favor active management—will behave?

A problem in disguise is the "opportunity" ETFs offer to invest in single markets or commodities. There are over 100 single-country ETFs and over 150 single-commodity ETFs and 200 leveraged or reverse-leverage ETFs. Unless you are a recognized expert or have a unique and specific reason to use one of the highly specialized ETFs, don't even begin to think about it.

The pattern by which innovations win acceptance is well known. The short description is simple: slowly and inevitably. The process is one of resistance being overcome one person at a time. Resistance to innovation—the viscosity of acceptance— differs by society: farmers were slow to accept the innovation of hybrid seed corn; doctors were much less slow to accept new kinds of pharmaceuticals; and teenage girls are quick to take up the new, new anything. Two groups are important:

- Innovators are always trying new things. Their experiments often fail, but they delight in the newness and do not mind

the failures because they never overinvest in their experiments and don't take it personally if the new thing fails.
- Influentials are widely respected for their ability to pick new ways with high rates of success and almost never fail.

Interestingly, Influentials monitor Innovators closely, and when they see an experiment succeed, they will then try it too. Because the Influentials only try what has worked for the Innovators, their success rates are very high. That's why they are influential: many, many people watch what they do and follow them with confidence.

ETFs and indexing are—at a curiously slow pace—moving up the familiar curve of acceptance and are doing so at a gradually accelerating rate. Why? Because more and more investors are realizing that ETFs and indexing have been and surely will be consistently more successful—after fees, costs, and taxes (and after adjusting for risk)—than active management. Is this a slam on active managers? Certainly not! In fact, it is only because active managers are so talented, hardworking, and well armed with databases, computers, Bloombergs, access to the research of CFAs, and many other advantages, and are so clearly dominating stock market activity, that indexing works so well.

In reality, the supreme compliment to active management is ironic: it is only because so many active managers are so good that the market they produce—while certainly not "perfect"—is now so very efficient. Market efficiency is due to so much talent working so hard and so skillfully to get it right that almost no active managers are able to do better than the expert consensus—particularly after fees.

Active manager fees are quoted as "only 1 percent" of assets, but the investor already has all those assets. So what are fees as a percentage of returns? If returns average 7 percent (as many now expect in the low-growth world ahead), then fees are about 15 percent of returns. And as all economists remind us, the real cost of active management is that the incremental fee for active investing is a percentage of incremental returns greater than the "commodity" offering: index funds. That means incremental fees for active investing (over the widely available index alternative) are now over 100 percent of incremental returns. Increasingly, the unhappy results of active management—after fees—are causing clients to have serious questions about the cost-benefit value of active investment management.

Given the persistent accumulation of evidence, there should be little wonder that we are seeing more and more institutions and individuals using ETFs and indexing, and no wonder that institutions and individuals who are already using ETFs and indexing are steadily increasing their allocations. The real wonder is why the two rates of increasing demand are not even greater.

As all grandparents and most parents know (and as most grandchildren will come to know), the real test of a good driver is simple: no serious accidents. And as all fliers know, safe, dull—even boring—is the essence of a good flight. The secret to success in investing is not in beating the market any more than success in driving is going 20 miles over the posted speed limit. Success in driving is being on the right road and moving at a reasonable speed, with no accidents.

Success in investing comes from having clearly defined objectives and the right asset mix and staying with the program. ETFs and indexing make it easier for investors—institutions and individuals—to focus on what really matters: setting the right goals on risk, designing the portfolio most likely to achieve those sensible objectives, rebalancing as appropriate, and staying the course. Indexing and ETFs simplify policy implementation, freeing the investor to focus on long-term goals, portfolio strategy, and investment policy. That's why indexing and "plain vanilla" ETFs are increasingly important for individuals and institutions correctly interested in winning the winner's game and not losing the loser's game.

Notes

1. A few active managers have an above-average probability of outperforming over the long term. Each of them is unusual. One group consists of meticulously proficient "super quants." But while we are all inspired by their success, we cannot understand their process and so are unable to identify the few that will succeed (and that are accepting new outside clients). Another group of outperformers are small research firms that have small numbers of stocks and very low turnover because they are long-term "Phil Fisher" investors devoted to isolating out-of-favor but truly great companies. These firms are hard to find.
2. Berkshire Hathaway Annual Report, 1996.

CHAPTER 6

INVESTOR RISK
AND BEHAVIORAL
ECONOMICS

POGO, THAT FAMOUS FOLK PHILOSOPHER, SHREWDLY OBSERVED an essential truth that has particular meaning for investors: "We have met the enemy and he is us." So true! In the same vein, George J. W. Goodman, writing as "Adam Smith," wisely cautioned, "If you don't know who you are, the stock market is an expensive place to find out." We are emotional because we are human. We believe that we'll do better when we try harder. We find it hard to take advice such as "If it ain't broke, don't fix it." Because we're human, we are not even close to being entirely rational. So if an investor does harm, we need to know how and why.

Investing can usefully be understood by dividing it into three parts: the market, the investment manager, and the investor. All too many investors—unfortunately for themselves and their overall long-term investment experience—assume that the investment manager has the leading role, that the market and all its gyrations come next, and that the individual plays only a minor part. Actually, the true order of importance is exactly opposite: today the *investor* has by far the most important role, and the investment manager has the least important role (Figure 6.1).

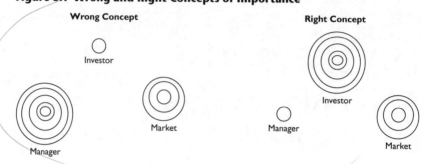

Figure 6.1 Wrong and Right Concepts of Importance

Fifty years ago, active managers did perform the most important roles, but due to the confluence of numerous important changes, the role an active manager can perform successfully has declined over the years to a rather small one. Ironically, this profound diminution is not because of any loss of skill or drive among active managers. On the contrary, it is only because so many brilliant, ambitious, hardworking professionals have been attracted to investing that they have collectively made it nearly impossible for any one of them to outperform the collective consensus on price discovery. And that's why—even though it takes even greater skill to be competitive in today's market—the investment manager's proper role has become smaller and smaller.

On the positive side, because each investor is unique, only the investor—often with help from an investment advisor—can specify that investor's unique set of goals, based on that investor's risk tolerance, investment expertise, present and future financial resources, and present and future financial obligations, responsibilities, and personal aspirations.

Most investors, most investment managers, and *all* advertisements about investments focus on only one side of investing: returns. There is another side: *risk*—particularly the risk of serious permanent loss. And for long-term success, that other side is even more important than returns. Risk comes in various forms: Madoff, Enron, WorldCom, and other deliberate frauds and scams; Polaroid, Lucent, and other companies that saw their shares fall as their businesses suffered unexpected troubles; individual investors getting frightened out of the market at a terrifying low and not getting back in before the market recovers; trying too hard and buying into stocks or a fund at a market peak; investing in your employer's stock out of loyalty and therefore not being wisely diversified; or running out of retirement funds because you did not save enough or invested unwisely or spent too much or "lived too long." Losses—not market fluctuations but real, permanent losses—are destructive, both financially and spiritually. The risk of such losses is clearly the real risk.

In a Wall Street training program, one participant brashly asked the distinguished and wealthy senior partner how to "get rich like you." After a long pause, the answer came back: "Don't lose!" Many of the trainees thought, "If you ask a dumb question, you deserve a dumb answer." But 50 years later, they all had learned that *not losing* was really important. When you're down 50 percent, you need a *double* just to get even.

For many years, economists operated on the assumption that people are rational calculators, know what they want to achieve, know how to achieve it, and consistently strive to make rational, unemotional, self-interested decisions in order to achieve their objectives. More recently, behavioral economists have shown that, as human beings, we are not always rational and we do not always act in our own best interests. Investor risk comes in many guises that have been noted by students of behavioral economics. Here are some of the things we actually do:

- We fail to appreciate the great power of regression to the mean.
- We ignore the "base rate," or normal pattern of experience. (Even though we *know* the odds are against us, we gamble at casinos and get caught up in bull and bear markets.)

- We believe in "hot hands" and winning streaks and that recent events matter, even in flipping coins. (They do not.)
- We overreact to first impressions, so we allow our initial views to anchor our future thinking and distort our analysis of subsequent information so that our conclusions confirm our first impressions.
- We suffer from an illusion of control and underestimate the odds of bad events—particularly very bad events.
- We evaluate the quality of a decision based on the favorable or unfavorable outcome, not on the quality of the way the decision was made. This is called either "hindsight bias" or "outcome bias."
- We overrely on experts—and are overconfident of their expertise.
- We respond to the "halo effect" of a recommendation from someone we admire, even in an area outside the person's turf, such as athletes endorsing particular soft drinks, watches, or travel destinations.
- We overweight dramatic events that are easy to recall or events that are given extensive media coverage.
- We overestimate our own skills and our own knowledge.
- We are overly impressed by short-term results like recent mutual fund performance.
- We are "confirmation biased," looking for and then overweighting the significance of data that support our own initial impressions.
- We anchor our final judgment to an early estimate even when we know it was "just a number."
- We distort our perceptions of our decisions, almost always in our own favor, so we believe we are better than we really are at making decisions. And we don't learn; we stay overconfident.
- We confuse familiarity with knowledge and understanding.
- We overreact to recent good news and to recent bad news.

- We think we know more relative to others than we really do. (And nearly 80 percent of us think we are "above average" as car drivers, as listeners, as dancers, at evaluating other people, at being friends, on having a good sense of humor, as parents, and as investors. And 80 percent of us quietly believe our children are also above average.)

We now know that as human beings we are endowed with certain inalienable characteristics of mind and behavior that compel us to make imperfect decisions—even dreadfully serious mistakes—as investors. We often do not realize how we think and react, so we would be wise to use simple checklists to guide our behavior—just as Captain Sullenberger so wisely did when, shortly after takeoff, his engines stopped and he suddenly had to land his plane in the Hudson River.

"At least, let's not do it to ourselves," urged JFK. His caution about self-inflicted harm applies to all investors because we ourselves cause risks that are quite unnecessary and could easily be avoided if we would just recognize our unfortunate proclivities and discipline ourselves to do less harm, particularly to ourselves and our investments. Benign neglect can be good for us as investors.

Here are some of the investor's risks to avoid:

- *Trying too hard* and taking too much market risk.
- *Not trying hard enough*—usually by having too much in money market funds or bonds.
- *Being impatient.* If your investments went up 10 percent a year, that would be less than 1 percent a month. On a *daily* basis, that rate of change would be anything but "interesting." (Test yourself: How often do you check the prices of your stocks? If you check more than once a quarter, you are satisfying your curiosity, not your need for price information.) If you make an important investment decision more than once every year or so, you are almost surely being too active in trading.

- *Changing the mutual funds you own after less than 10 years.* If you're doing this, you're really just "dating." Investing in mutual funds should be *marital*—entered into soberly and advisedly and for the truly long term. Changing mutual funds costs investors heavily. The average return realized by mutual fund investors is sharply lower than the returns of the very funds they invest in just because investors sell funds with recent disappointing performance and buy funds with recent superior performance. As a result, we all too often sell low and buy high, repeatedly throwing away a significant part of what we could have earned if we had only shown enough patience and persistence.
- *Borrowing too much.* Three out of four of the fortunes that are lost get lost because borrowed money was used. The borrowers were hoping to make an even bigger pile, but it became a painful "pileup" instead.
- *Being naively optimistic.* Being hopeful is often helpful in other fields, but in investing it's much better to be objective and realistic.
- *Being proud.* Over and over again, studies show that we substantially overestimate our own investment capabilities and our investment performance relative to the market. And we don't like to recognize and acknowledge our mistakes—even to ourselves. Too often, we are also stubborn. Remember the adage: "The stock doesn't know you own it." And it really doesn't care.
- *Being emotional.* We smile when our stocks go up and frown or kick the cat when our stocks go down. Our feelings get stronger and stronger the more, and the faster, the prices of our stocks rise or fall.

Our internal demons and enemies are pride, fear, greed, exuberance, and anxiety. These are the buttons that Mr. Market most likes to push. If you have them, that rascal will find them.

No wonder we are such easy prey for Mr. Market and all his attention-getting tricks.

The crucial question is not simply whether long-term returns on common stocks would exceed returns on bonds or T-bills if the investor held on through the many startling gyrations of the market. The crucial question is whether the investor *will*, in fact, hold on for the long term so that the expected average returns can actually be achieved. The problem is not in the market but in ourselves, our perceptions, and our all-too-human short-term reactions to our present perceptions.

This is why it is so important to develop a realistic understanding of investing and of capital markets, so Mr. Market will not trick you—and to develop a realistic knowledge of your own tolerance for market fluctuations and your long-term investment objectives, so you won't trick yourself. The more you know about yourself as an investor and the more you understand the securities markets, the more you will know what long-term asset mix is really right for you and the more likely it is that you will be able to ignore Mr. Market and sustain your investment commitments for the long term.

Investor risk can be reduced, often quite substantially, in four ways: avoiding all-too-human operational mistakes; carefully determining your own *realistic* investment objectives; designing a sensible long-term strategy to achieve your particular objectives; and staying committed to your long-term program. (When deciding on your investment program, be sure to ponder carefully how you might have been tempted to react to unusual markets—both unusually favorable and unusually unfavorable—in the past. Unusual events will come again.)

That's why the best way to start learning how to be a successful investor is to follow the standard instruction: know thyself. As an investor, your capabilities in two major realms will determine most of your success: your intellectual capabilities and your emotional capabilities.

Your *intellectual capabilities* include your skills in analyzing financial statements (balance sheets, funds flow accounts, and income statements); the extent and accuracy of your ability to store and recall information; how extensively you can correlate and integrate various bits of data and information into insight and understanding; and how much knowledge you can master and use about hundreds of different companies and their stocks.

Your *emotional capabilities* include your ability to be calm and rational despite the chaos and disruptions that will, thanks to Mr. Market, intrude abruptly upon you and your decision making.

Each investor has a zone of competence (the kind of investing for which he or she has real skill) and a zone of comfort (the area of investing in which he or she will be calm and rational). If you know yourself—your strengths *and* your weaknesses—you will know the limits you must learn to live with in each realm. The place where your spheres overlap in a Venn diagram (see Figure 6.2) is your investor's sweet spot. That's where you want to concentrate: where you have the right skills *and* the right temperament to do your best investing. (In the trade-off between the conflicting investor goals of "eat well" and "sleep well," the sage advice is to "sell down to the sleeping point.") Don't go outside your zone of competence because you'll make costly mistakes. And don't go outside your comfort zone because you may get emotional, and being emotional is never good for your investing.

Figure 6.2 The investor's Venn diagram

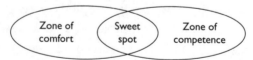

Zone of comfort — Sweet spot — Zone of competence

A strong defense is the best foundation for a strong offense in investing, so always stay inside your comfort and competence zones. It is *your* money, so treat it with the care and respect it deserves and you deserve, investing only when you know from experience that you have the requisite skill *and* can be consistently rational.

Investing is a process. Good investing comes from a very good continuous process and, as in every continuous process, if anything commands an observer's attention, there is a problem with the process. A good continuous process should never be "interesting."

CHAPTER 7

YOUR "UNFAIR" COMPETITIVE ADVANTAGE: INDEXING

ALL GREAT STRATEGISTS SEEK TO ESTABLISH A SUSTAINABLE advantage over their competitors. That's why:

- Army generals want to take the high ground and have the advantage of surprise.
- Coaches want stronger, taller, faster players; strive for ever-better conditioning; and care a lot about team spirit and motivation.
- Corporate strategists attempt to create "branded" franchises for their products and services and try to build strong brand loyalty among each group of customers.
- Corporations strive to move up the "experience curve" so their unit costs of manufacturing will be lower than those of any competitors. Patent protection, FDA approval, low-cost transportation, technological leadership, consumer preferences, and trademarks all have one thing in common: competitive advantage.

In each case, strategists are trying to identify and obtain a significant, sustainable, strategic advantage—what competitors will feel is an "unfair" competitive advantage. In investing, there are three ways to achieve a desirable unfair competitive advantage.

The *physically* difficult way to beat the market is the most popular, or at least the most widely used. Believers in this game plan get up earlier in the morning, stay up later at night, and work on weekends. They carry heavier briefcases and read more reports, make and take more phone calls, go to more meetings, and send and receive more e-mails, voice messages, and text messages. They strive to do more and work faster in the hope that they can get ahead of the competition.

The *intellectually* difficult approach to beating the market is used by only a few investors, including a very few whose skills inspire us all. They strive to think more deeply and see further into the future so they can gain truly superior insight and understanding of particular investment opportunities.

The *emotionally* difficult approach to superior investing is to maintain calm rationality at all times, never get excited by favorable market events, and never get upset by adverse markets. This should be the easiest way to invest. But at market extremes, who among us actually finds it easy to sustain that most useful investment stance, benign neglect?

You are well suited to the "easy" way if you can examine the facts of the situation and accept the conclusion that your own efforts are unlikely to improve on accepting reality, and acknowledge the fact that your efforts are unlikely to improve matters. We all do this with weather conditions. As more investors are learning when investing in today's highly professionalized markets, accepting the consensus of experts at low cost by indexing is wise.

The *easy* way to gain, and sustain, an unfair competitive advantage as an investor is to invest in index funds. If you can't beat 'em, join 'em. An even better reason for individuals to index is that when you do, you are then free to devote your time and energy to the one role where you have a decisive advantage: knowing yourself and your own particular objectives so you can accept markets as they are and concentrate your drive and skills on designing a long-term portfolio structure of stocks, bonds, and other investments that will meet two important tests:

- You can and will live with the market risks of this portfolio— even at their extremes.
- The long-term expectable results will meet your objectives.

The great advantage of indexing investment operations is that we can avoid the vain search for superior performance and concentrate our time and energy on investment policy and asset-mix decisions. Instead, it focuses your attention on the most important decision in investing: defining the long-term "policy" portfolio that will both minimize the risk of avoidable mistakes and maximize the chances of achieving your true investment objectives.

While some professional investors are so skillful and so independent minded that they really can add value by actively changing their investments, the record shows repeatedly that their number is fewer than most investors want to believe. More important, the chances of your identifying one of the great winners *before* the record has been established is very low. Finally, most of the great winners are not accepting new money from new investors.

Changing managers effectively—firing one before disappointment comes *and* hiring a new one before success is shown—is virtually impossible. For many years, data have shown that most investors get it wrong both ways. At pension funds, the fired manager's future results are usually better than the newly hired manager's. Recent studies document that the same problem applies to individual investors.

If, as the pundits say, "success is getting what you want" and "happiness is wanting what you get," you can be both successful and happy with your investments by concentrating on the right asset mix and by living with a few simple truths so your investments really will work for and serve you and your purposes. Most individual investors make many mistakes over many years and go through many unhappy experiences to learn these simple—but never easy—truths. Fortunately, there is a convenient alternative: we can all learn by reading history. Markets are markets and people are people. Together they have created a lot of history. Market history will repeat itself because it's so hard for people as a group to learn or change.

Here are the "unfair" advantages of index investing in today's market environment:

- Higher rates of return because over the very long term, 80 percent of active managers fall short of the market. It's nearly impossible to figure out ahead of time which managers will make it into the winning top 20 percent—and, long-term, most of these will not stay winners.
- Lower management fees and expenses: fees of 10 basis points (0.1 percent) or less versus 100 to 120 basis points (1.0 to 1.2 percent)—compounding year after year.
- Lower taxes. Fewer profits are recognized each year—particularly as short-term gains—because turnover is so much lower. For actively managed mutual funds, tax costs average about 1 percent of assets every year, so saving that "just 1 percent" can increase your rate of return—and that's 15 percent more than today's expected annual returns of only 7 percent in your pocket every year.
- Lower brokerage commissions because portfolio turnover is a lot lower: below 10 percent per year for indexing versus more than 60 percent for actively managed mutual funds.
- Lower "market impact" costs of transactions because portfolio turnover is so much lower.
- Convenience. There are almost no records to keep.

- And best of all . . . freedom from numerous modest errors or even a major blunder, because no market timing or portfolio strategy decisions and no manager selection decisions are required—all decisions that can so easily go wrong—and because no single stock ever represents a disproportionate position in your portfolio.
- Freedom to focus on *really* important decisions like your investment objectives and sensible long-term investment policies and practices that will work well for you.

The case for indexing accumulates greater and greater strength as the period for evaluation lengthens. Performance problems for actively managed funds come episodically and over time. Over the longer term, as experts with skill, tenacity, and drive increasingly dominate the markets, markets will surely become more efficient. So trying to beat the market will continue to get harder.

* * * * *

To minimize risk relative to return—or to maximize return relative to risk—investors should at least consider fully diversifying internationally. Most investors are surprised to learn that the best plain-vanilla index fund mix is about half domestic and half *international*. Recognizing that diversification is the investor's single "free lunch," it's easy to see that investing proportionately in all the world's major stock markets and all the different economies those markets represent significantly increases diversification. That's why wise investors choose an index fund that replicates the broadest market at low cost.[1] For entirely rational investors, this will be a worldwide "total market" index fund.

Investors who decide to concentrate their investments in their home country are making an implicit decision to emphasize that one country over others. Curiously, most investors do just that. British investors concentrate their investments in the United Kingdom. Canadian investors focus on Canada, Japanese investors on

Japanese stocks, Australian investors on Aussie stocks, and New Zealanders on Kiwi stocks. They may be right to do so only if their home country has a large, complex, and dynamic economy like that of the United States *and* they have large financial obligations or responsibilities in that country's currency.

Exchange-traded funds have mushroomed in assets and proliferated in number and variety since the first one was introduced in 1993. There are now more than 2,000 ETFs and ETPs with total assets of over $3.4 trillion. Investors should know that most of the growth in ETFs has not come from individual investor demand but from dealers and professionals hedging against particular risks, not investing for the long term.[2]

There are index funds and ETFs for every major market around the world (and for the whole world stock market) as well as for small caps or large caps or growth or value portfolios. However, although each index is designed to replicate a market or a sector of the market fairly and accurately, indexes are *not* all created equal.[3] Usually, the differences are small and inconsequential, but in some markets, differences among indexes—and the index funds that track them—are significant, particularly in the fees charged.[4]

* * * * *

Warren Buffett once estimated what he considered the annual "horrendous costs" of active investing to be:

- Over $40 billion for trading just the shares of Fortune 500 companies at 6 cents per share.
- $35 billion for management fees, expenses, sales charges, wrap fees, and so on.
- $25 billion for a miscellany of spreads on futures and options, costs of variable annuities, and the like.

Noting that all this was "just" 1 percent of the total market value of the Fortune 500, Buffett, always seeing reality as an owner should, reminded us that this $100 billion cut a big chunk out of the $334 billion that the whole Fortune 500 earned that year. As a result, investors earned less than $250 billion—just 2.5 percent—on their investment of $10 *trillion*. That 2.5 percent return on investment was, in Buffett's view, "slim pickings." Don't we all agree?

Another "leak" in an individual investor's return comes with taxes driven by portfolio turnover. The more turnover, the more taxes and the lower the accumulated returns. (With short-term gains, which are often realized in mutual funds, the negative impact of higher taxes is even greater.)

If you decide to "overweight" small cap stocks or emerging markets or even frontier markets in your portfolio structure, you can do so with index funds, ETFs, or both. But beware: The argument for index funds is strongest when investing in the most efficient markets, like those for large cap stocks in the United States, the United Kingdom, and Japan. Specialized index funds and specialized ETFs invest in markets that are not as broad, deep, and efficiently priced. In smaller markets, market replication is more difficult and less accurate. Still, in every major market, index funds achieve better performance than most of the actively managed funds investing in those same markets.

Notes

1. Costs are deducted from dividends on the underlying shares, with the remainder paid out semiannually. (Dealers make profits on commissions, on securities lending, and on the float between receipt of dividends from underlying companies and semiannual payouts to holders of ETFs.)
2. More than 95 percent of ETFs and 85 percent of ETF assets are specialized. Professional investors, particularly at hedge funds, use these ETFs to fine-tune risk management. Normal investors should never use them.

3. More than 200 index funds are now available, including 50 different S&P 500 funds. But not all S&P 500 index funds are equal. Some charge much more than others do.
4. Buyers beware: Virtually identical index funds can have costs that are three times higher—for no added value. ETFs also differ significantly in expense ratios, which can range from 0.05 percent to 1.60 percent—an 80-to-1 ratio.

CHAPTER 8

THE PARADOX

A PARADOX IS HAUNTING ACTIVE INVESTMENT MANAGEMENT: funds of investors with very long-term purposes are all too often *not* being managed to achieve long-term objectives that are feasible and worthwhile. Instead, they are being managed to meet short-term objectives that may be neither feasible nor important.

The unimportant and daunting task to which most active managers devote most of their time—with little success—is trying to beat the market. Realistically, outperforming the equity market by even close to one-half of 1 percent *consistently*, without taking above-average market risk, would be a great success that almost no sizable investment organizations have achieved for long. Ironically, and painfully for both individual and institutional investors, managers who strive to *beat* the market almost all come in behind the market indexes.

The truly important but not very difficult task to which investors and their investment managers could and should devote themselves involves four steps:

1. Understand each investor's real investment objectives.
2. Define realistic risk and return investment policies to meet those real objectives.
3. Establish the asset mix or portfolio structure best suited to achieving those risk and return objectives.

4. Develop the self-discipline to stay on a well-reasoned investment plan as markets move and even gyrate.

(For a more forceful explanation of how major changes over
the past 50 years make low-cost indexing today the best way for
almost all investors to invest, please read *Index Revolution*, published by John Wiley and Sons. This work is a winner's game,
and *everyone* can be a true winner.)

At every ski resort, the trails are marked by degree of difficulty so each skier can go to the right slopes. Beginners know the
bunny slopes will be smoothly groomed, with no ice patches or
bumps, and will be perfect for slow and easy skiing. And 17-year-
old heroes with spring-steel legs and 100 days a year of skiing
can chase one another down the double black diamond expert
runs. If they each go to the trails that are right for them, thousands of skiers can enjoy the mountain at the same time. (If the
17-year-old gets stuck on the beginner's slope or Grandma goes
to "double black," both will suffer!)

The same arrangement works for different kinds of investors *if*
they are realistic about themselves and realistic about the kind of
investment portfolio that's right for each of them. We are different from one another in many ways. Here are a few:

- Age
- Assets
- Income
- Time horizon
- Dependents
- Investment experience
- Risk tolerance
- Likely inheritance
- Intended bequests
- Philanthropic aspirations

Chances are, nobody is quite the same as you or me—or any other specific investor. (Our fingerprints, DNA, and eyes all differ from everyone else's too.) What's best for each investor is probably unique. That's why each investor should tailor his or her investment portfolio so it's really right for her or him.

The best opportunity to achieve superior investment results lies not in scrambling to outperform the market but in establishing and adhering to appropriate investment policies that enable you to reach *your* objectives by riding with the main long-term forces in the market over time and through market cycles.

In reality, few investors have developed clear investment goals, so most investment managers operate without really knowing their clients' specific objectives and without explicit agreement on their mission as investment managers. *This is the investor's fault.* While investment counseling is more important to long-term success than investment management and can make far more economic difference over the long term, most investors do not do the disciplined work of formulating sound long-term investment policies for themselves. That's why—for relatively modest fees—investment counseling is the most important investment service most investors will ever use.

Getting it right on investment policy, with or without a professional advisor, is up to you, the investor. After all, it is your money. You know the most about your overall financial and investment situation: your earning power, your ability to save, when you plan to retire, your obligations for your children's educational expenses, the likely timing and scale of needs for spendable funds, and how you feel about the disciplines of investing. Only you can know your own tolerance for changes in market prices, particularly at market extremes, when the pressures for change are strongest. So it's your responsibility to know who you really are as an investor and what you really want. While responsibility can be foolishly *abdicated*, final responsibility should not be delegated. Still, investors can get great help from fee-only financial advisors on how best to think through the answers to six important questions.

First, what are the real risks to you of an adverse outcome, particularly in the short run? Unacceptable risks should never be taken. For example, it would not make sense to invest all of a high school senior's college tuition savings in the stock market—if the market went down, the student might not be able to pay the tuition bill. (Education is a great long-term investment, but the bill must be paid when received.) Nor would it make sense to invest in stocks all the money saved for a house just two or three years before the intended date of purchase.

Second, what are your probable emotional reactions to an adverse market experience? You should know this and stay well within your tolerance—ideally, a well-informed tolerance—for interim price fluctuations in your portfolio. Avoiding market risk does have a real opportunity cost. That's why you should understand all the gains and losses that must be anticipated with each incremental level of market risk taken—and the opportunity cost of each level of market risk *not* taken.

Third, how knowledgeable are you about the history and realities of investing and the realities and vagaries of financial markets? Smart investing does not always make sense except in retrospect. Sometimes astute investing seems almost perversely counterintuitive. Lack of knowledge tends to make investors too cautious in bear markets and too confident in bull markets—all too often at considerable cost. Suggestion: go to your library and spend several hours reading the daily newspapers from the summer and fall of 1929, the fall of 1987, the dot-com era, or the fall of 2008. Getting "up close and personal" can help you understand how it feels to be in a storm and may help you learn how to remain calm in the next one.

An investor who is well informed about the investment environment will know what to expect. He or she will be able to take in stride the disruptive experiences that may cause other, less informed investors to overreact to either unusually favorable or unusually adverse market experiences.

Fourth, what other capital or income resources do you have, and how important is your investment portfolio to your *overall* financial position?

Fifth, are there any legal restrictions on your investments? Many trust funds are quite specific. Many endowment funds have restrictions on how income is to be defined and spent.[1]

Sixth, are there any unanticipated consequences of interim fluctuations in portfolio value—possibly rather large ones—that might affect your optimal investment policy?

Each of these possible concerns should be studied so that the investor can ascertain how much deviation from the normally optimal investment policy—broad diversification at a moderately above-average market risk—is truly warranted. We all know that it can be hard for individual investors to continue taking the long-term view when markets are rising rapidly or, worse, falling rapidly.

By defining your objectives, you can focus on what really matters: not the futile struggle to beat the market, but the reasoned and highly achievable goal of setting and meeting your own realistic long-term investment objectives.

If investors are not willing to act like principals, we can be sure that the paradox—managing *long-term* investments according to *short-term* priorities—will remain in force for a long, long time. Individual investors have an important opportunity to achieve an optimal match between their long-term investment objectives and the long-term investment strategy that's best for each of them.

Cynical observers of the paradox that haunts investment management say it is unrealistic to expect investors to take on the self-discipline of doing all that homework or to expect investment managers to risk straining client relationships by insisting on a well-conceived and carefully articulated investment policy with explicit objectives when most investors seem uninterested in going through the discipline.

So escaping from the paradox depends on you asserting your role as the expert on your own needs and resources and developing appropriate investment goals and policies. For that important work, while we can get real help from experienced financial advisors, we must look primarily to ourselves.

Note

1. As William Carey and Craig Bright advocated in *The Law and the Lore of Endowment Funds* (1969), perceived restrictions should be carefully examined because they may not, in fact, be as confining as they may initially appear.

CHAPTER 9

TIME

TIME IS ARCHIMEDES'S LEVER IN INVESTING. ARCHIMEDES IS often quoted as saying, "Give me a lever long enough and a place to stand, and I can move the earth." In investing, that lever is time (and the place to stand, of course, is on a firm and realistic investment policy). Time—the length of time investments will be held, the period over which investment results can be measured and judged—is crucial to any successful investment program because it is the key to getting the right asset mix.

Time transforms investments from *least* attractive to *most* attractive—and vice versa—because while the average expected rate of return is not at all affected by time, the range or distribution of *actual* returns around the expected average is greatly affected. Given enough time, investments that might otherwise seem unattractive become highly desirable—and vice versa.

The longer the time period over which investments are held, the closer the actual returns in a *portfolio* will come to the expected average. (The actual returns on *individual* investments, in contrast, will often be more and more widely dispersed as the time period lengthens.) As a result, time changes the ways in which portfolios of different kinds of investments can best be used by different investors in different situations and with different objectives.

If time is *short*, the highest-return investments—the ones a long-term investor naturally most wants to own—will *not* be desirable, and a wise short-term investor will avoid them. But if the time period for investing is abundantly *long*, a wise investor can commit without great anxiety to investments that in the short run would appear to be too risky.

The conventional time period over which rates of return are usually calculated—their average *and* their distribution—is just one year. What a shame! While convenient and widely used, this 12-month time frame simply does not match the time periods available to all the different kinds of investors with all their different constraints and purposes. Some investors are investing for only a few days at a time, while others will hold their investments for several decades. The difference in the time horizon matters greatly in investing. To show how important time is, let's exaggerate for effect and look at the returns expected for a *one-day* investment in common stocks.

If a typical stock's share price is $40, the range of trading during one day might easily range from $39.25 to $40.50—a range of $1.25, or 3.1 percent of the average price for the day. Remembering that the average annual rate of return for common stocks in recent decades has been approximately 8 percent, let's postulate that an investment in this hypothetical stock would have an expected daily return of 0.04 percent (8 percent annual return divided by 250 trading days each year) and a range around that expected average of plus or minus 1.55 percent (the 3.1 percent intraday range divided by 2).

Now let's "annualize" that daily return of 0.04 percent and that daily price variation. The average annual expected rate of return would still be 8 percent, but the *range* of returns around that 8 percent would be a daunting plus or minus 387.5 percent! In other words, the annualized rate of return for a one-day investment in our hypothetical stock would be somewhere between a *profit* of 395.5 percent and a *loss* of 379.5 percent!

Of course, no sensible investor would knowingly invest in common stocks for only a single day or a month or even for a year. Such brief time periods are clearly too short for investments in common stocks because the expectable *variation* in return is too large in comparison to the expected average return. The extra uncertainty incurred when investing in common stocks is not balanced in the very short run by a sufficiently large or sufficiently sure reward. Such short-term holdings in common stocks would not be investments; they would be rank speculations.

However, this deliberate one-day burlesque of the conventional use of annual rates of return leads to a serious examination of the differences in investor satisfaction when the measurement period is changed. That examination shows why an investor with a very long time horizon might invest entirely in common stocks just as wisely as an investor with a very short time horizon would invest only in Treasury bills or a money market fund. The examination also shows why an intermediate-term investor would, as his or her time horizon is extended outward, shift investment emphasis from money market instruments toward bonds and then more substantially toward equities.

Despite the constancy of the average *expected* rate of return—no matter what the time period—the profound impact of time on the actual *realized* rate of return is clearly demonstrated in the chart in Figure 9.1. The one-year-at-a-time rates of return on common stocks over the years are almost incoherent. They show both large and small gains and large and small losses occurring in a seemingly random pattern. At best, you could have earned 53.4 percent in a year, but at worst you could have lost 37.3 percent. It seems almost absurd to "summarize" those wildly disparate one-year experiences as having *any* "average" rate of return.

Shifting to five-year periods brings a considerable increase in regularity. There are, for example, few periods with losses, and the periods with gains appear far more often and consistently because, as the measurement period lengthens, the long-term average rate of return increasingly dominates the single-year differences.

Figure 9.1 Range of returns of stocks, bonds, and "cash" after adjusting for inflation

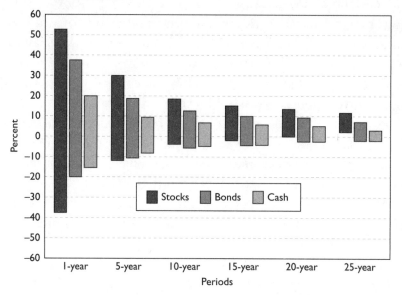

Shifting further to 10-year periods increases the consistency of returns. Only *one* 10-year loss is experienced, and most periods show average annual gains of 5 to 15 percent. Again, the power of the "base rate" average rate of return, now compounded over a full decade, overwhelms the single-year differences.

Moving on to 20-year periods brings even more consistency to the rate of return. There are no losses, only gains. And the gains cluster more closely together around the long-term expected average rate of return.

Appreciating that actual experiences in investing are all samples drawn from a continuous stream of experience is vital to understanding the meaning contained in the data. Even in New England, the weather—when considered over a long time—becomes a sensible, reliable *climate* even though the days of bitter cold or sweltering heat seem individually so unpredictable, particularly in regard to the exact dates of their occurrence. Similarly, in investing, the patient observer can see the true underlying patterns that make the seemingly random year-by-year, month-by-month, or day-by-day experiences *not* disconcerting or confusing but splendidly predictable—on average and over time.

In weather and investments, larger and more numerous samples enable us to come closer and closer to defining the nature of the normal distribution from which the sample is drawn. This understanding of the normal experience allows you to control your own behavior so you can take advantage of the dominant long-term normal pattern and not be thrown off by the confusing daily events that present themselves with such force in the short term as Mr. Market strives to catch your attention.

The single most important dimension of your investment policy is the asset mix, particularly the ratio of fixed-income investments to equity investments. Analyses of asset mix show repeatedly that the trade-off between risk and reward is driven by one key factor: time.

Lamentably, the time horizon most often used is not chosen for the specific investor but is instead a conventional five years. This usually leads to the familiar recommendation of a 60:40 ratio of equities to debt. A 10-year horizon usually leads to an 80:20 ratio. A 15-year horizon typically results in a 90:10 ratio. And so it goes. The unfortunate reality is that none of these time horizons is right for most individual investors who want to provide financial security for their families. They are all far too *short* for an investor with a realistic investment horizon of 30 to 50 years or more—most investors will be living and still investing for more than the conventional 10 to 20 years. If more investors used truly long-term thinking, they would invest differently and would earn higher long-term returns.

CHAPTER

RETURNS

INVESTMENT RETURNS COME IN TWO VERY DIFFERENT FORMS: quite predictable cash received from interest or dividends and quite unpredictable—at least, in the short run—gains or losses in market price. Investors who devote most of their time and skill to trying to increase returns by capitalizing on changes in market prices—by outsmarting other investors—are making a big mistake.

Changes in market price are caused by changes in the consensus of active investors about what the price of a stock ought to be. This consensus is determined not by individual investors but by many thousands of professional investors constantly seeking opportunities for investment profit. To find these opportunities, professional investors:

- Study monetary and fiscal economics and political developments in all the major nations
- Visit hundreds of companies and attend thousands of breakfast, lunch, and dinner meetings with corporate executives, economists, industry authorities, securities analysts, and other experts
- Study reports and analyses produced by several hundred companies and dozens of large brokerage firms
- Read extensively in the industry and trade press

- Talk almost constantly on the telephone with people who have ideas, information, or insights
- Use Bloomberg and access the latest information via the Internet

In addition to studying the *rational* world, professional investors also study the irrational world of behavioral economics and investor psychology, consumer confidence, politics, and overall "market tone," because in the short run the markets, thanks to Mr. Market, are not entirely rational. The ways in which investors perceive and interpret information and the ways they react to developments impact market prices, particularly in the short run. Therefore, professional investors are always looking for opportunities to capitalize on changes in other investors' opinions before changes in their own opinions are capitalized on by other investors.

Even with all this homework, of course, not all the interpretations and perceptions of professional investors are correct. Some, particularly in retrospect, will seem terribly wrong. But the process of thousands of highly motivated professionals all striving to discover the correct prices is very hard to beat.

Active investment management in today's dynamic markets is a turbulent, fascinating, hopeful, anguishing, stressful, and sometimes euphoric process of competing—in the world's most free and competitive market—against many talented and ambitious competitors for any advantages that might be gained from greater knowledge, wiser interpretation, or better timing.

The irony is that for most investors, professional or individual, most of this activity really does not matter—not because the investment professionals are not highly talented but because so many competitors are *equally* highly talented.

For all the surface complexity in the process, two main areas are dominant in evaluating common stocks. The first is the consensus of investors on the probable amount and timing of future earnings and dividends. The second is the consensus of investors on the discount rate at which this stream of estimated future dividends and earnings should now be capitalized to establish its present value.

Estimates of future dividends and earnings will vary among different investors and at different times due to changes in expectations for long-term economic and industry growth, cyclical fluctuations in unit demand, prices, taxes, discoveries and inventions, competition at home and abroad, and so forth. Over time, the discount rate considered appropriate will also vary with many factors, among which the most important are the perceived risk of a particular investment or investments of its general type or the expected rate of inflation. In addition, active investors know that other investors' estimates of other investors' estimates of still other investors' estimates ad infinitum are always changing and that a third set of estimates—how other investors' estimates of others' estimates *will* probably change—is always changing too, sometimes greatly.

The longer the future period over which estimates of earnings and dividends *and* of the discount rate are extended, the greater the uncertainty that will be factored into investors' estimates of other investors' estimates, driving day-to-day, month-to-month, and year-to-year fluctuations in stock prices.

Note that the consensus that matters for long-term investors is not today's consensus about the distant future but the consensus that will prevail when we actually get to that distant future. As the holding period over which an investor owns an investment lengthens, the importance of the discount factor decreases and the importance of corporate earnings and paid dividends increases.

For a very long-term *investor*, the relative importance of earnings and the dividends received is overwhelming. For a short-term price *speculator*, everything depends instead on the day-to-day and month-to-month changes in investor psychology.

Like the climate, the average long-term investing experience is never surprising. But like the weather, the short-term experience is *frequently* surprising.

Long-term investors understand from experience the remarkable discipline of normal distribution of the bell curve of economic behavior and events and the strong tendency of major forces in the economy and the stock market to move toward "normal" via regression to the mean. They know that the farther current events are from the center of the bell curve, the stronger the forces of regression to the mean pull current experience back toward the center or average.

Such mean reversion characterizes the physical world too. Sailors know the remarkable power of the "righting arm" in which the farther the boat heels, the harder the keel works to keep it upright. Similarly, it is more likely that tomorrow's temperature will be *less* hot and that the children of unusually tall people will *not* be as tall as their parents.

Investors want to know the most probable investment outlook for the years ahead. One way to look ahead is to appraise the likely *change* in two powerful variables: long-term interest rates and corporate profits. To be realistic, assume that the future range of interest rates and profits will be within the historical upper and lower limits and will tend toward their respective means. *Caution:* if the market has been going up, investors, who usually evaluate future prospects by looking into the rearview mirror, will assume some upward momentum. And if the market has been trending down, they will add some downward momentum. The wise investor will adjust for this notorious human tendency.[1]

The history of returns on investment, as documented in study after study, shows three basic characteristics:

- Common stocks have average returns that are higher than those of bonds. Bonds in turn have higher returns than short-term money market instruments.

- The daily, monthly, and yearly fluctuations in actual returns on common stocks exceed the fluctuations in returns on bonds, which in turn exceed the fluctuations in returns on short-term money market instruments.
- The magnitude of the average period-to-period fluctuation in rate of return increases as the measurement period is shortened and decreases as the measurement period is lengthened. In other words, rates of return appear more normal over longer periods of time.

While daily and monthly returns show virtually no predictive or predictable pattern, they are not really random. Hidden within Mr. Market's gyrations is a strong tendency of regression to the mean rate of return. That's why investment managers are learning to describe investment returns in formal statistical terms. Individual investors would be well advised to learn enough about the language of statistics to have an awareness of what is meant by *mean* and *normal distribution* and what is meant by *two standard deviations* as a measure of the frequency with which unusual events are expected and do occur.

In addition to learning the importance of describing the distribution of returns around the mean, we have learned to separate out the different components in the average rate of return and to analyze each component separately. The average rate of return has three main components:

- The *real* risk-free rate of return
- A premium over the risk-free rate of return to offset inflation's *expected* erosion of purchasing power
- A premium over the inflation-adjusted risk-free rate of return to compensate investors for accepting market risk

Dividing total returns into these three classes of return makes it possible to compare the returns of these types of investments:

stocks, bonds, and Treasury bills. This work has been done in a series. The analysis is informative.

Treasury bills appear quite safe and reliable—in nominal terms, not adjusted for inflation—with apparently positive returns in almost all years. However, when adjusted for inflation, returns are positive less than 60 percent of the time. Even more startling, the average annual rate of return on Treasury bills after adjusting for inflation is zero.

In other words, Treasury bills are usually no more than a match for inflation. Most of the time, you do get your money back, with its purchasing power intact. But that is all you get. There is virtually no real return *on* your money, just the return *of* your money (see Figure 10.1).

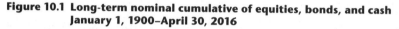

Figure 10.1 Long-term nominal cumulative of equities, bonds, and cash January 1, 1900–April 30, 2016

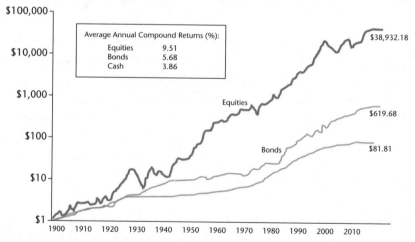

Sources: *BofA Merrill Lynch, Citigroup Global Markets,* Common-Stocks Indexes *(Cowles Commission), Global Financial Data, Inc., Standard & Poor's, and Thomson Reuters Datastream.*

Long-term bonds produce higher returns, inflation-adjusted, for two reasons: corporate bonds involve a risk of default, and both corporate and government bonds impose on the investor an exposure to market fluctuations caused by their more distant maturity, as the market continuously adjusts prices to changing expected interest rates. Investors don't want to experience the market price fluctuations unless they get a higher rate of return to compensate, so long bonds pay a higher rate of interest—a *maturity premium*. The maturity premium is estimated at 0.9 percent, and the default premium on high-grade long-term corporate bonds works out to about 0.5 percent. Adding these two premia to the risk-free rate, the inflation-adjusted annual real rate of return on long government bonds is a little above 1.0 percent in normal markets, and on long-term high-grade corporates it is usually nearly 1.5 percent.

It makes sense that returns on common stocks are higher than returns on bonds, which guarantee to pay interest and their full face value at maturity. Stocks make up for not having such guarantees with a risk premium built into their nominal returns. The inflation-adjusted expected real rate of return is about 5 to 6 percent. When the disruptive impact of inflation is removed and gains are examined over reasonably long periods, it becomes clear how consistent the returns investors require for their money really are. This consistency stems from two main factors:

- Investors are sensibly consistent in requiring higher rates of return to compensate them for accepting higher market risk.
- As the period over which returns are measured is lengthened, the short-term volatility in returns caused by fluctuating changes in the discount rate becomes less and less important and the expected dividend stream or interest payments, which are much more stable, become more and more important.

We do not have and cannot hope to get precise data on rates of return from investments in securities any more than we can expect to get "correct" data by sampling any other complex, dynamic, continuous process that is affected by a multitude of large and small exogenous factors. However, we can get a very useful *approximation* of what returns have actually been and what they are most likely to be, and that is all we really need to establish investment policies for the long term.

Unless you buy in at the start of the period measured, sell out at the end, *and* then take your money out of the market, performance data are simply representational statistics. They describe samples from a continuous and very long process in which stock prices go through a "random walk" series of successive approximations of the actual present value based on continuously revised estimates of future earnings and dividends and changing discount rates.

Two further propositions on returns are important. First, the impact on returns of changes in the *expected* level of inflation can be enormous, particularly on common stocks, which are virtually perpetual investments. Such a change in the expected rate of inflation from approximately 2 percent in 1960 to approximately 10 percent in 1980 (along with other changes) caused a change in the required nominal average rate of return from common stocks from about 9 percent in 1960 to about 17 percent in 1980, and this produced a major reduction in stock prices. From that reduced level, future returns would meet the returns after inflation that investors needed to justify buying stocks. Note that after factoring in the ravages of inflation, the losses investors experienced during that "adjustment" period were the worst in half a century. A decrease in the expected rate of inflation had the opposite effect, as we saw in the following 25 years of a bull market rise in stock prices.

The second proposition on returns is that differences in rates of return that may appear moderate in the short run can, with compounding (because interest is paid not only on the principal but also on the reinvested interest), multiply into very large and quite obvious differences in the long run. (When asked what he considered the human race's most powerful discovery, Albert Einstein allegedly replied without hesitation, "Compound interest!")

Figure 10.2 shows the compounding effect on $1 invested at different interest rates and compounded over different periods of time. It's well worth careful study, particularly to see how powerful time is.

That's why the Archimedes lever of investing is time.

Figure 10.2 How compound interest over time magnifies one dollar

	Investment period		
Compound rate of return	**5 years**	**10 years**	**20 years**
4%	$1.22	$1.48	$2.19
6	1.34	1.79	2.65
8	1.47	2.16	4.66
10	1.61	2.59	6.73
12	1.76	3.11	9.65
14	1.93	3.71	13.74
16	2.10	4.41	19.46
18	2.29	5.23	27.39
20	2.49	6.19	38.34

Before leaving the happy realm of investment returns, take another look at Figure 9.1 in Chapter 9, particularly the data on 25-year returns. The moderate levels of *real* returns (adjusted for inflation) are impressive and instructive: 6.6 percent for stocks and 1.8 percent for bonds.

After an extraordinary quarter century of generally highly favorable investment experiences, investors needed to remind themselves in the early years of this century of the normal, or "base," rate of investment returns. The high nominal returns of the prior quarter century were well above the base rate—as the losses in 2008 would so bluntly prove.

Beware of averages. If stocks return an average of 10 percent per year, how often over the past 75 years did stocks actually return 10 percent? Just *once*, in 1968. And how often did returns even come close to that specific number? Only three times. That's why investors need to "average" delightful and dreadful markets over many years. It's not easy.

The next time you feel excited by a zooming bull market, try to remember what airline pilots say are the two "strong expression" wishes of passengers. The first is when your plane is on the ground because of bad weather and you're anxious to get to an important meeting; waiting impatiently, you say, "I wish to God we were in the air." The second is when you are in the air in a major storm, saying, "I wish to God we were on the ground!"

Most investors do not want to preclude themselves arbitrarily from making the big score—the opportunity to "shoot the lights out."[2] If you believe with Louis Pasteur that "chance favors the prepared mind," be sure that you are prepared. First, be prepared to find nothing much.

In nearly 50 years of continuous active involvement with many of the world's best investors, I've found only two major opportunities that weren't obvious to many others. That's a discovery rate of only once every 25 years of nearly full-time searching.

If you find a great investment opportunity, what should you do?[3] Try asking four questions and then ask other people to examine your reasoning process with you:

1. What could go really *right*, and how likely is that?
2. What could go *wrong*, and how likely is that?
3. Am I so confident that I should invest a significant part of my portfolio in this one investment?
4. If the price goes down, will I *really* want to buy a lot more?

Notes

1. Warren Buffett used this straightforward approach near the millennium—when the consensus of investors was that they

actually expected nearly 13 percent annual average returns to extend the strong bull market for another 10 years—to show why he expected inflation-adjusted returns of only 4 percent annually. How right he was to be skeptical, again, of the cheery consensus!

2. *Fortune*, November 22, 1999.

3. My father loved bridge and played often. He was impressed one evening when, after three passes, his bridge partner opened with a preemptive bid: "Small slam in hearts!" He was astonished when his happy partner said, "It's a lay-down!" Dad was astounded as his partner showed his hand: it was all hearts! Aghast, Dad asked the obvious question, "Why didn't you bid *grand* slam?" He was not amused by the reply: "Since you had not bid, I wasn't sure how much support your hand would give me." The opportunity missed was too great to forget. Dad never forgot.

CHAPTER 11

INVESTMENT RISKS

*R*ISK IS SUCH A SIMPLE LITTLE WORD THAT IT IS AMAZING HOW many different meanings are given to it by different users. Risk is different from uncertainty. Risk describes the expected array of payoffs when both their magnitude and their probabilities of occurrence are *known*. Actuarial mortality tables are a familiar example. The actuary does not know what will happen in 14 years to Mr. Frank Smith, but she *does* know quite precisely what to expect for a group of 100 million people—in each and every year. "Riskiness" in investing, by contrast, is akin to *uncertainty*, and that's what the academics mean when they discuss beta (relative volatility) and market risk. Too bad they don't use the exact terms.

Risk exists both in the markets and in the individual investor. Market risk is in the price fluctuations that, over time, tend to cancel each other out. Investor risk—either euphoria and excessive confidence at peak prices or fear and panic at terrible market lows—can provoke actions causing permanent harm. Many of us can live fairly comfortably with most near-term market volatilities and resist the urge to take action, knowing that over the long run, more market volatility usually comes with higher average returns. But some cannot. For them, the great risks of wrong actions at the wrong times are imposed on themselves *by* themselves.

Active investors typically think of risk in four different ways. One is price risk. You can lose money by buying stock at too high a price. If you think a stock's price might be high, you *know* you are taking *price* risk.

The second type of risk is interest rate risk. If interest rates go up more than was previously expected and already discounted in the market, your stocks will go down. You are taking *interest rate* risk.

The third type of risk is business risk. The company may blunder, and earnings may not materialize. If this occurs, the stock will drop. Here you are taking *business* risk.

The fourth kind of risk is the most extreme: *failure* risk. The company may fail completely. That's what happened with Penn Central, Enron, WorldCom, and Polaroid. As the old pros will tell you, "Now *that* is *risk!*"

Real risk is simple: not enough cash when money is really needed—like running out of gas in the desert. Advisors wisely focus on the grave risk all investors, and 401(k) investors in particular, should focus on: running out of money, particularly too late in life to go back to work.

Another way to look at risk has come from the extensive academic research done over the past half century. More and more investment managers and clients are using it because there's nothing so powerful as a theory that works. Here's the concept: Investors are exposed to three kinds of investment risk. One kind of risk simply cannot be avoided, so investors must be rewarded for taking it. Two other kinds of risk *can* be avoided or even eliminated; investors are *never* rewarded for accepting these unnecessary and avoidable kinds of risk. And that's why we should all diversify.

The risk that cannot be avoided is the risk inherent in the overall market. This market risk pervades all investments. It can be increased by selecting volatile securities or by using leverage or borrowed money, and it can be decreased by selecting securities with low volatility or by keeping part of a portfolio in cash equivalents or bonds. But it cannot be avoided or eliminated. It is always there. So it must be *managed*.

The two kinds of risk that can be avoided or eliminated are closely associated. One involves the risk linked to individual securities; the other involves the risk that is common to each type or group of securities. The first can be called *individual-stock risk*, and the second can be called *stock-group risk*.[1]

A few examples will clarify the meaning of stock-group risk. Growth stocks as a group will move up and down in price in part because of changes in investor confidence and willingness to look more or less distantly into the future for growth. (When investors are highly confident, they will look far out into the future when evaluating growth stocks.) Interest-sensitive issues such as utility and bank stocks will all be affected by changes in expected interest rates. Stocks in the same industry—autos, retailers, computers, and so forth—will share market price behavior driven by changing expectations for their industry as a whole. The number of common causes that affect groups of stocks is great, and most stocks belong simultaneously to several different groups. To avoid unnecessary complexity, investors usually focus their thinking on the major forms of stock-group risk.

The central fact about both stock-group risk and individual-stock risk is this: they do not need to be accepted by investors; they can be eliminated. Unlike the risk of the overall market, the risk that comes from investing in particular market segments or specific issues can be diversified away, almost to oblivion.

That's why in an efficient market no incremental reward can or will be earned over the market rate of return simply by taking either more individual-stock risk or more stock-group risk. Either type of risk should be incurred only when doing so will enable the investor to achieve truly worthwhile increases in returns.

The lack of reward for taking individual-stock risk or stock-group risk is important. An investor who takes such risks can hope to be rewarded only by superior skill in selecting individual stocks or groups of stocks that were somehow inappropriately priced. As explained in Chapter 3, an investor who takes these risks can profit only if competitors—now almost always experts—make mistakes. This is not an encouraging basis for making a major commitment.

Fortunately, such risks can be avoided by using the simple and convenient strategy of investing in index funds that replicate the market. No deviations in portfolio composition relative to the overall market means no deviations in rate of return and no stock-group risk or individual-stock risk. An index fund provides a convenient and inexpensive way to invest in equities with the riskiness of particular market segments and specific issues diversified away.

Note that eliminating these two particular forms of risk does not mean that all risk is gone. Overall market risk will always be there, and in the field of risk, that's the big one. Figure 11.1 shows vividly how the riskiness of a single stock consists primarily of individual-stock risk and stock-group risk, but it also highlights that due to diversification in a typical portfolio, these two kinds of risk are only a small part of the investor's total risk.

The figure also shows that the typical index funds investor will have even more diversification, which will further reduce the specific-issue and market segment risks. Investors who add international index funds get still more diversification.

The optimal level of market risk for a very long-term investor is moderately above the market average. This makes sense because most other investors are not free to take a very long-term view. Many know their investments will be liquidated sooner—for their children's education, at the termination of a trust, or for a host of other near- to medium-term events for which plans must be made. Other investors are simply unable to look with calm forbearance on the abrupt and substantial day-to-day, month-to-month, and year-to-year changes in stock prices that will be experienced in an equity portfolio over the long term. These investors want less risk and less fluctuation and are willing to pay a price—by giving up some incremental return—to get what they want.

Figure 11.1 How diversification reduces nonmarket risk

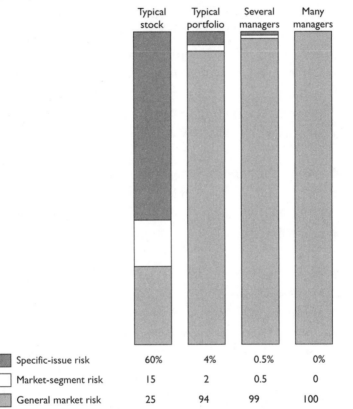

	Typical stock	Typical portfolio	Several managers	Many managers
Specific-issue risk	60%	4%	0.5%	0%
Market-segment risk	15	2	0.5	0
General market risk	25	94	99	100

In summary, the total return to an equity investor has four components:

1. The risk-free return after offsetting expected inflation
2. An extra return to compensate for the riskiness, or price uncertainty, of investing in the overall equity market

3. A potential extra return for investing in one or more particular groups of stocks or market segments that for various
   economic, business, or market psychology reasons may
   behave differently from the overall market
4. An additional potential extra return for investing in specific
   stocks that, for the same sorts of reasons, may behave differently from the overall market.

Corresponding to each component of *return* is a component of
risk. In investment management, we now know that the crucial
factor is not how to manage rates of return but how to manage
market risk. By managing market risk, we are doing two things
at the same time:

1. Deciding deliberately what level of market risk to establish
   as the portfolio's basic policy
2. Holding to that chosen level of market risk through good
   and bad markets

Changes in the level of market risk should be made only
because the investor's long-term objectives have changed.

Managing market risk is the primary objective of investment
management. That is a profound assertion, and it is the core idea
of this chapter. The rate of return obtained in an investment portfolio comes from three sources, in this order of importance: first
and foremost, the level of market risk assumed or avoided in
the portfolio; next, the consistency with which that risk level is
maintained through market cycles; and last, the skill with which
specific-stock risk and stock-group risk are eliminated or minimized through portfolio diversification.

The difference between true investment risk and apparent riskiness or market risk is a function of time. Yes, stocks can be very
risky if time is short. But unless you begin your investment program at a silly "too high" level in the stock market, the apparent

riskiness of stocks fades away if the time is long enough, and the favorable long-term returns become increasingly evident. If you're not confident that the market is low, you'll be wise to use dollar-cost averaging (investing a fixed dollar amount at regular intervals) to get gradually invested over time.

For investors, investment risk can also be divided by *time* into short-term risk versus long-term risk. The real risk in the short term is that you will need to sell to raise cash when the market happens to be low. That's why in the long term the risks are clearly *lowest* for stocks, but in the short term, the risks are just as clearly *highest* for stocks.

One risk that most investors are not prepared for is how long it can take for the stock market to recover to peak prices. It's worth remembering that it took 16 years for the S&P 500 stock index to get back up to its 1966 peak and even longer to regain the peak of 1929. But if you do not need to sell and don't sell, you really shouldn't much care about the nominal fluctuations of stock prices. They may be interesting, but they aren't any more relevant to you than stormy weather in faraway places or low tide on the high seas.

Because the real risks in the long run are the risks created unnecessarily by their reactions, investors' best answer to short-term market riskiness is to ignore the interim fluctuations and be patient, persistent, long-term investors. Risk tolerance does not describe the behavior we expect of ourselves when calmly considering normal markets, long-term averages, or the normal volatility of returns. Risk tolerance calibrates our behavior when we are driven by real worries during market extremes, particularly after we've recently been proven wrong—again. To the extent that you know your investments will be held for the very long term, you have automatically self-insured against the uncertainty of short-term market price fluctuations. As long as you stay invested, the interim price fluctuations of Mr. Market will not cause you serious harm.

Recognizing that investment risk drives returns and is not simply a residual of the struggle for higher returns transforms our concept of investment policy. We now know to focus not on rate of return but rather on the informed management of risk.

Note

1. Academic writers use slightly different terms to describe these three types of risk: market risk is called *systematic risk*, individual-stock risk is called *specific risk*, and stock-group risk is called *extra market risk*. The terms used here seem clearer and more natural.

CHAPTER 12

BUILDING PORTFOLIOS

WHETHER INVESTING IS PRIMARILY AN ART OR A SCIENCE HAS long been a favorite topic of informal discussion among professional investment managers, perhaps because the discussions typically are resolved quite cheerfully by demonstrating that since the practice of investing is clearly not a science, it must be an art.

Anyone who has observed gifted investors at work will recognize the art—subtle, intuitive, complex, and almost inexplicable—in selecting individual stocks or groups of stocks. The few great artists are true heroes of the profession who add value to portfolios by seeing and seizing opportunities others miss or recognize only later.

However, for most investment managers, portfolio management is neither an art nor a science. It is instead an unusual problem of engineering. The great lesson of engineering is that the key to finding the solution is to define the real problem correctly. When you have defined the problem correctly, you are well on your way to finding the correct solution. Portfolio management is investment engineering. Working within a remarkably uncertain, probabilistic, and always changing world of partial information and *mis*information, all filtered through the inexact screen of human interpretation, determines the most reliable and efficient way to reach a specified goal, given a set of policy constraints.

While certainly far from perfect, recent advances in the availability of information, the power of computers, and the development of modern portfolio theory are providing investment managers—and their more sophisticated clients—with the tools and concepts they need to understand and define investment problems so they can be managed toward "best available" solutions. (It would be a naive presumption to believe that the problems of managing an investment portfolio can be "solved.")

As explained in Chapter 11, we now know that the real challenge in long-term investing is not how *to increase returns*—presumably by buying low and selling high—but how *to manage risk* by deliberately taking appropriate levels of market risk that will lead over time to moderately increased returns.

Good portfolio design eliminates avoidable and unintended risk and maximizes expected returns at a deliberately chosen level of market risk. This produces an *efficient* portfolio. An efficient portfolio has greater expected returns than any other feasible portfolio, with equal risk and less risk than any other feasible portfolio with equal expected returns.

Once an efficient portfolio has been constructed at the level of risk that is appropriate for a particular investor, it would not make sense to incur more individual-stock risk or stock-group risk unless such risk was directly associated with a specific opportunity to capture significant extra return.

The amount by which market risk and return can be magnified in a portfolio by investing in moderately more price-volatile stocks is certainly not spectacular, but the benefits over the very long run can be worthwhile. (A portfolio with a market risk that is 20 percent greater than the overall market average is feasible. A market risk much higher than that would be difficult to design into a portfolio while keeping the portfolio well diversified. The number and variety of stocks needed to achieve good diversification *and* provide that much additional market risk are simply not available in the market.)[1]

Thus far, our discussion has concentrated on equity investments. Portfolio management for bonds is different in the details, but the main concepts are much the same. Like stocks, bonds present both individual risk and group risk that can and should be diversified away. For example, bonds issued by companies in a particular industry will, as a group, change in value with major changes in that industry's economics.[2] Bonds sharing particular call or refunding features will rise and fall in relative market popularity as a group. The normal difference in yield (and therefore price) between corporate and government bonds changes, causing larger or smaller spreads between corporates as a group and governments as a group.

Bond rating agencies have found that most of their rating errors are caused by the difficulty inherent in estimating such *group* risks, not in estimating the individual risk of a particular issuer compared with other issuers in the same industry or group. Sadly, this was proven again in 2008, when triple-A credit ratings were given to newly issued securities backed by subprime mortgages. The rating agencies were seriously wrong *systematically* on group risk, which led to enormous losses for investors relying too much on Moody's and S&P ratings. (Credit rating mistakes have happened many times before—starting with triple-A-rated street railways in the 1920s. Virtually all went bankrupt as people switched to automobiles.)

Conceptually, bond portfolio management starts with a passive portfolio that represents the overall bond market. This baseline portfolio is diversified across numerous groups and across individual issues to protect against the credit risk of individual issuers or types of issuers, and it uses an evenly spaced schedule of maturities to defend against adverse changes in interest rates. As with equities, the historical evidence is that the risk of individual bonds can be substantially reduced through diversification. Portfolios of medium- to lower-grade issues do, after absorbing all actual losses through defaults, provide higher net returns over time than portfolios of higher-grade issues. That's why portfolio managers with direct access to superb proprietary credit research can increase risk-adjusted returns while concentrating on mispricing among lower-grade bonds.

Individual investors should never buy individual corporate bonds; diversification is an absolute necessity in bond investing to ensure the return of your money. Fortunately, well-managed bond funds of all types are now available at low cost. How much to invest in bonds, and whether to invest in bonds at all, not which particular bonds you invest in, will be the most powerful determinant of your overall results.

As it has been for fiduciaries since the invention of insurance and pooled risk accounts in merchant shipping on sailing vessels hundreds of years ago, the basic responsibility of mutual fund managers and all investment professionals is to prevent surprises and control portfolio risk in deliberate pursuit of wisely determined and explicitly stated long-term investment objectives. Most active investors see their work as assertive and on the offensive. But today the reality is that stock investing and bond investing are and should be primarily *defensive* processes. The great secret to success in long-term investing is avoiding serious, permanent loss.

The saddest chapters in the long history of investing tell tales of investors who suffered serious losses they brought on themselves by trying too hard and succumbing to greed. Leverage is all too often the instrument of self-destruction. Investors will be wise to remember the great difference between *maximization* and *optimization* as they decide on their long-term strategy. Icarus was a maximizer, as were many of history's destroyed "fortune builders" who, like Hamlet's hapless military schemer, got hoist with their own petards.[3]

Notes

1. A 20 percent increase on a 7 percent overall market return on equities would be 1.4 percent incremental return.
2. The catastrophic collapse of mortgage bonds in 2008 was a dramatic and painful illustration.
3. A petard was a small bomb or land mine.

CHAPTER 13

WHOLE-PICTURE FINANCE

MONEY, AS WE ARE TOLD IN ECONOMICS 101, IS FUNGIBLE. YET most investors think of their investment portfolios as standalone entities, separate from their other assets. This is a major mistake because the wrong framing will almost certainly lead to unnecessary worries as securities markets fluctuate. It will also lead to asking the wrong questions, getting the wrong answers, and making the wrong decisions by not seeing the whole financial picture.

Here's one example: Conventional wisdom says we should invest our age in bonds. But is that sensible? Should a 30-year-old MBA actually put 30 percent of her investment portfolio in bonds? Not if you reframe the question to include her largest financial reality: the present value of her earned income for the next 35 to 45 years.[1]

So how might she think today about her expected future income? With a little effort, the most probable earnings progression can be sensibly estimated. (She could check with her company's human resources department, her business school, or executive search firms.) Then she could convert that stream of annual expected incomes into their net present value.

Without much effort, we know the first words she'll use when she sees the number: "Wow! Huge! My goodness!" (And this ignores her probable opportunities for stock options or bonuses *or* investing savings to earn further returns. It also leaves out any pension or 401(k) plan and Social Security benefits.)[2] As an asset, the net present value of her future salary earnings will tower over her current investment portfolio.

The asset mix of her "whole picture" portfolio will be loaded with the capitalized value of her future earnings and will be over 95 percent of her total financial portfolio. So why should she "invest her age" in still more bonds? Surely she shouldn't! Her securities portfolio should be at least 100 percent in stocks.[3] (She might even go over 100 percent by using moderate margin leverage in her all-equity portfolio.)

Over time, other components of her whole-picture portfolio will gradually become important. For example, there's a high probability she will have a nice home. If she's thinking in terms of her whole picture, she will include her home as well as the net present value of her future earnings and not make the mistake of thinking of her securities portfolio in isolation from her other present and future assets. Also, when stocks go up and down, she will be wise to practice thinking of her whole financial picture, which will be changing much less than the part invested in stocks. So she need not worry as much as her cohorts who compartmentalize their assets into subgroups and fret too much about the relatively volatile behavior of one part of the whole picture. Chances are she does not need to own bonds to achieve "balance." Over the long term, whole-picture thinking will enable her to invest more in stocks and—over the very long term, possibly half a century—earn a significantly higher total rate of return.

The whole-picture portfolio includes capitalized Social Security benefits[3] as well as the value of a pension fund or 401(k). These assets are certainly part of the whole financial portfolio each of us should be seeing in its totality. (If she is anticipating an inheritance, that too should be recognized as she thinks through her overall financial situation and plans.)

Notes

1. Retiring at 65 will no longer be the social norm when she gets there, and she may, like me, want to keep working because it's so interesting.
2. Some advisors would recommend owning some bonds to give her investment portfolio a "stabilizing balance." This may be wise for some investors, but they should recognize this reality: the lower rate of return on bonds can be a high cost to pay for "anxiety insurance." It may be cheaper to devote more time and effort to understanding markets and learning how to live with volatility.
3. Those approaching the "zone of retirement" will be wise to give careful consideration to another part of whole-picture financial management—the substantial advantages of not claiming Social Security benefits until age 70. The financial advantages of continuing to work can be compelling.

CHAPTER 14

WHY POLICY MATTERS

THE PRINCIPAL REASON WE SHOULD ALL ARTICULATE OUR LONG-term investment policies explicitly and in writing is to protect our portfolios from ourselves. The discipline helps us adhere to our long-term plans when Mr. Market misbehaves again and makes current markets distressing and puts our long-term investment policies suddenly in doubt. Misdemeanors in investing are almost all the result of our inadequate advance understanding of the *internal* realm of our own short-term emotions in response to abrupt changes in the *external* realm of capital markets or specific investments, or both.

All too often, investment policy is vague, implicit, and left to be resolved in haste when unusually distressing market conditions are piling pressure on. That's when it is all too easy to make the wrong decision at the wrong time for the wrong reasons.

Such hasty decisions can result in investors selling stocks *after* they have dropped steeply in value and then missing the subsequent recovery in the equity market, and vice versa: buying stocks at or near the market's high when the record *looks* most compelling. Such ill-timed changes in the asset mix have been severely harmful to investors' long-term returns.

Technology has been transforming investing, albeit not as much as GPS (global positioning system) technology has transformed navigation. Thanks to new technology, investment managers can approximate—within the array of feasible results—the intended long-term "relative to market" level of risk for any particular portfolio. Investors now have every right to expect results that match their reasonable risk expectations *and* their fund managers' capabilities. With investment operations conveniently indexed, investors can focus on developing long-term policies that will, over time, achieve specified goals within each investor's tolerance for interim market risk.

The best shields against the disruption of Mr. Market's short-term provocations are knowledge and understanding, particularly knowledge of yourself and your own goals and priorities. That's why your carefully considered investment strategy should be committed to writing. Don't trust yourself to be completely rational when all those around you are being driven by emotion, because you are human too.

As an investor, you will be winning when the results you want are the results you get by following the long-term policies that match your personal long-term priorities.

In theory, we all know our long-term interests are best served by lower stock prices—so we can all buy more shares at bargain prices. But who among us is delighted by falling markets? And who does not feel a warm glow of affection for stocks and markets that have gone up, even though we know it means that stocks are now more expensive to buy and future rates of return on additional investments at these higher price levels will surely be lower?

By contrast, who among us would close our pocketbook and turn away from the store that puts its most attractive wares on sale at 10, 20, or even 30 percent off its recent prices? None of us would say, "I don't want to buy these things when they're on sale; I'll wait until the price goes back up and then buy." But that's exactly how most of us actually do behave with investments.

When the market drops, putting stocks "on sale," we stop buying. In fact, the record shows that we even join in the selling. And when the market rises, we buy more and more enthusiastically. As market expert Jason Zweig puts it, "If we shopped for stocks the way we shop for socks, we'd be better off." We are wrong when we feel good about stocks having gone up, and we are wrong when we feel bad about stocks having gone down. So we should keep reminding ourselves that a falling stock market is the necessary first step to our buying low.

Psychologists who study anxiety and fear have found that four characteristics make people more worried about the perceived riskiness of a situation than the realities would warrant: large-scale consequences, a lack of personal control or influence, unfamiliarity, and sudden occurrence. As a result, we are more fearful of air travel (in which fewer than 30 people are killed and far fewer than 350 are hurt in a typical year) than of automobile travel in the United States (in which 45,000 people are killed yearly and well over 350,000 are seriously injured).

Most investors experience great anxiety over large-scale, sudden losses in portfolio value primarily because they were not informed in advance that such events are part of how markets sometimes behave. Sharp losses are to be expected and even considered *normal* by those who have studied and understand the long history of stock markets.

Such drops in the market are predictable—not in their timing, of course, but in their probable magnitude and suddenness. No wonder nonstudents experience attacks of anxiety. It is in these periods of anxiety, when the market has recently been most severely negative, that investors allow their short-term fears to overwhelm the calm rationality that is best for long-term investing.

Investors can get inundated by information in written reports from economists and stock analysts and by telephone calls and e-mails on market transactions that give a compelling urgency to the here and now *and* to what others are or may be thinking of doing. The resulting excessive attention to the present not only produces "groupthink" mistakes, but it also distracts our attention from the long-run nature of successful investing.

Investors need protection from their human proclivities toward unrealistic hopes and unnecessary fears, provoked by the emotionally compelling experiences of positive or negative surges in the market and by the current opinions that drive them. This is understandable. Investors who are not sufficiently informed about the true nature of investment markets *will* get surprised. Severe, sudden storms—such as the financial world experienced in 2008—surprise almost everyone. And investors' collective reactions to surprise in turn surprise almost everyone else. That's what creates panic.

We can substantially improve our long-term investment returns by being sure we understand—as much as we can—the realities of the investment environment in which our portfolios operate. Thoughtful, objective study of the past is the best and least costly way to develop an understanding of the basic nature of markets and, in particular, the nature of market extremes. That's why it pays to study market rates of return and patterns of deviation from the averages over the past several decades, learning as thoroughly as possible why markets move as they do.

As an investor, it is more rewarding to study investment history than to study the present market activity or estimates of the future. We don't want to get caught in Santayana's trap: "Those who cannot remember the past are condemned to repeat it." Again, visit your local library and read the financial section of your favorite magazine or newspaper for 1973, 1987, 1962, 1928–1929, 1957, 2000, and 2008. As Yogi Berra said, "It's déjà vu all over again." Markets always have been and always will seem surprising because every market is different in its details. But the major characteristics of markets are remarkably similar, time after time.

Only by understanding the nature of investing and capital markets will you escape the paradox in which too much attention is paid to daily market happenings and too little attention is devoted to the truly important work of developing and adhering to wise, appropriate investment policies and practices that can, over time, achieve better results for you—much better than most investors will enjoy.

CHAPTER 15

PLAYING TO WIN

THE WINNER'S GAME IN INVESTING IS OPEN TO *ALL* INVESTORS, so *every* investor can be a real winner—and it's almost easy. Almost. The first secret for success is that each investor has to ignore the "beat the market" hype that pervades the advertising that floods out of brokerage firms, actively managed mutual funds, and the investment letters from stock market gurus working in cahoots with Mr. Market.

The second secret for success is that each investor must decide for himself or herself what investment policies will, over the long term, have the best chance of producing the particular results he or she most wants to achieve. These winning investors are not in competition with one another; they are in competition only with themselves. Can they stay "on policy" even when Mr. Market goes into his gyrations? Investment policy is the explicit linkage between your long-term investment objectives and the daily operational work of investing. If policy is *not* determined through carefully developed understanding, it *will* be determined by improvisation or "adhocracy."

While most investors think of investing as an enormously complex blend of activities, it is easy and worthwhile to unbundle investing into five *separate* levels of decisions each investor can make:

- *Level One.* Settling on your long-term objectives and your asset mix: the optimal proportion of equities, bonds, and perhaps other assets to achieve *your* objectives.
- *Level Two.* Deciding on equity mix: the right proportions of various types of stocks—growth versus value, large cap versus small cap, domestic versus international. Same with bonds. (If you have a large portfolio, the same decisions can be made for subcategories of each major asset class.)
- *Level Three.* Choosing either active management or indexing to implement your policy mix of investments. As we have seen, for most investors index funds will be the best long-term choice.
- *Level Four.* Deciding which funds or managers will handle each component of your overall portfolio (where most investors, unfortunately, concentrate most of their time and effort).
- *Level Five.* Selecting specific securities and executing buy and sell transactions.

The least costly *and* the most valuable decisions are made on Level One: getting it basically right on long-term goals and asset mix. The last two levels—selecting specific managers and buying and selling specific securities—are the most expensive *and* the least likely to add value. (In addition, taxes and operating costs are much higher with the extra activity that comes from trying harder.)

Here's the ultimate irony of the loser's game: we are all too often dazzled by the excitement of the action and the chance to win on Level Five—Mr. Market's favorite territory—where the costs to play are high and the rewards are small. Even worse, the search for ways to beat the market distracts us from focusing on Level One, where the costs are low and the rewards can be large—very large.

Because almost any asset mix can be achieved through low-cost indexing, investors considering active management should have an objective basis for deciding that the actual incremental returns—not just the promises—will fully justify the extra cost and risk of selecting active managers. (See Chapter 21 for a discussion of fees.)

If, instead of using index funds, you wish to select an active investment manager who deliberately differentiates his portfolios from the market, you must take the time to understand clearly *how* he will differentiate his portfolios (whether by betting heavily on a few stocks, for example, or by favoring a particular stock market sector); *when* he will do so (whether continually as part of a long-term strategy or occasionally as a short-term tactic); and, most important, *why* he is confident that he will achieve favorable incremental results by taking these actions. If you're thinking of making these exceedingly difficult decisions yourself as an individual investor, please think again. In today's investment school of hard knocks, the tuition is high and the benefits are low.

Time, as we have seen, is the single most important factor that separates the appropriate investment objective of one portfolio from the appropriate objectives of other portfolios. The key is the length of time over which the portfolio can be and will remain committed to a sustained investment policy and over which you will patiently evaluate investment results versus your objectives and policies.

Many investors wisely want to have a reserve for current spending—a "cushion for caution" to separate their long-term investment portfolios from their regular expenses so they can sustain long-term commitments to their long-term advantage. The amount of this dedicated reserve should be carefully determined and not allowed to influence the much larger long-term investment portfolio. While you may want your reserve fund very liquid, cash positions within the *investment* portfolio should be minimized and most likely kept at zero.

Your personal income requirements are excluded from this discussion of investment policy because the rate of return for an investment portfolio cannot be increased just because you want more money to spend. It is indeed a foolish idea that the investment objective for a portfolio could or even should be set according to how much the investor wants to spend each year. Sometimes this perverse idea shows up in pension funds where the actuarial assumption about the rate of return is put forth as a "guide" to investment management. Sometimes it shows up when college presidents insist on higher endowment income to make up for operating deficits. And sometimes it arises when individuals try to force their retirement funds to finance a more expensive way of life than the funds can sustain.

In all its forms, this practice is nonsense. Spending decisions shouldn't influence investment decisions; it should be the other way around. Spending decisions should most definitely be governed by investment results—which follow from investment policies and the market's returns—because, frankly, the market doesn't give a damn what you *want* to spend.

From time to time, perhaps once every two or three years, it will be appropriate to make a systematic examination of your overall resources, your spending objectives, your market experience, your risk tolerance, and your investment time horizon—all key factors in establishing your investment policy.

Here are a few simple tests for every investment policy:

- Would the policy, if implemented, achieve your long-term objectives?
- Is the policy written so clearly and explicitly that a professionally competent stranger could manage the portfolio *and* conform clearly to your true intentions?
- Would you have been able to sustain a commitment to the policy during the most troubling markets of the past 50 years—including 2008?
- Is the policy realistically designed to meet your real needs and objectives as a long-term investor?

Sound investment policies will meet *all* these tests. Do yours?

CHALLENGES WITH PERFORMANCE MEASUREMENT

Y OU UNDERSTAND ALL YOU REALLY NEED TO KNOW ABOUT THE most important characteristics of investment performance statistics when you accept as obvious the following proposition: if many people are in a coin-tossing contest, you can predict two results with great confidence:

1. In the long, long run, most coin tossers will average about 50 percent heads and 50 percent tails.
2. In the *short* to intermediate term, however, some of the coin tossers will appear to be somewhat better than average at tossing heads—or tails—and a very few will appear to be *much* better than average.

If we were to inspect the record, surely the data on each individual coin tosser would be clear and objective. But we'd know better than to think that the *past* results would be good predictors of *future* results in coin tossing. Sooner or later, each of the coin tossers would inevitably become more and more average. As we've seen, statisticians call this powerful yet common phenomenon "regression to the mean." Understanding the determining power of regression to the mean is the key to understanding a lot about reported investment performance.

That is the challenge. Investment skill—unlike skill in other competitive activities, such as chess or poker—is exceedingly hard to measure because the process is so complex and involves so many different variables that can only be estimated. While investment management is a continuous process, it takes a long time to evaluate because specific investing problems differ from day to day as companies change and industries evolve in many different ways; the economy, government, and market environments differ from year to year; and the competition from other investors changes. Meanwhile, every investment manager ages, while firms accumulate assets to manage, add or lose people, access new technologies, change ownership, and so forth. By the time a masterful manager can be identified with reasonable certainty, the chances are high that she or he has changed significantly too. Since there is little or no stability in investing, a large sample of experience—which means a really long time—is needed to achieve reasonable substantial accuracy.

After careful statistical analysis, quantitative expert Barr Rosenberg estimated that it would require 70 *years* of observations to show conclusively that even a large 2 percent annual incremental return—a very large, seldom seen 20 percent increase over a large 10 percent base rate—was the result of superior active investment management *skill* rather than *chance*. (The "performance" statistics cited in most advertisements are all too often short-term samples of just a few years drawn from a most unusually complex, dynamic, and *continuous* process.) The stocks and bonds in the portfolios frequently change, companies and their businesses are always changing, and the factors that most affect the prices of securities (fear, greed, inflation, politics, economic news, business profits, investors' expectations, and more) never cease to change.

In a typical 12-month period, about 40 percent of mutual funds will beat the market (and even after taxes, 30 percent or more will so succeed). But can they succeed again and again over the next 10 or 20 years—or even longer? Historical data says, "No. Not likely." As an investor, you will be investing for a very long time. You know that changing managers is notoriously fraught with costs and risks, so you would want to stay with one superior manager *if* you could. But the lesson of history is that apparently superior active managers seldom *stay* superior for very long.

As long as your investment portfolio is not being cashed in, this multidimensional, turbulent set of change forces will go on and on. There are no real or final "results" until the process stops and the portfolio is liquidated.

Warning: performance measurement is least useful when it is needed most—and is needed least when it could be most effective. Performance data are based on too short a time period (too small a sample) to provide enough information to make an accurate, objective evaluation. And performance results for longer periods, which offer greater assurance of accuracy, are not sufficiently timely to be useful for current decisions. By the time performance data are good enough for investors to act with confidence, the optimal time for action will be long past.

Measurements of investment performance do not, at least in the short run, mean what they say. Performance measurement services do not report "results." They report only statistical estimates. As usually reported—with two-decimal "precision" for a specified time period—investment returns seem almost microscopically accurate: "Over the 12 months ended June 30, manager A returned 7.53 percent." Such articulated precision gives performance numbers the *appearance* of legitimacy. They do not deserve it. They are in truth only a small sampling, not a measurement, of a long-term series of investment returns. So, as small samples, they should be treated as statistics, with their lack of certainty fully shown with plus-or-minus boundaries.

A form of Gresham's law ("bad money drives out good") can easily take over as both fund managers and investors allow the obsession with short-term performance to drive out thoughtful consideration of longer-term investment practices and objectives. By expressing recent short-term returns in such precise terms, performance measurement may turn our heads and make us believe that the short term is meaningful *and* that the long term will resemble it. It almost never does. That's why short-term thinking—Mr. Market's specialty—is the mortal enemy of long-term investment success.

Regression to the mean is a central reality of the patterns observed in long time series of data (such as investment results and coin tossing). The active manager whose favorable investment performance in the recent past *appears* to be proving that he or she is a better manager is often—not always, but all too often—about to produce below-average results. Why? Regression to the mean! Usually, a large part of the apparently superior performance was not due to superior skill that will continue to produce superior results, but was instead due to one sector of the market temporarily enjoying above-average rates of return—or luck.

When the tide turns, the behavior of the segment of the market that propelled the active manager ahead may now hold him or her back. That's one reason mutual fund managers' results so often regress to the mean. Another reason is this: with so many professional investors who are so good at what they do, it is difficult for any one of them to beat the crowd continuously at price discovery—the essential key to superior performance—because the crowd is full of well-informed, intensely competitive, and disciplined professionals who play the same game with the same information technology and the same constraints.

Long-term performance data of active managers will almost always have both a "survivor bias" and a backdating, or "new firm," bias. As we saw in Chapter 10, the resulting combination of these two kinds of bias can create dangerously deceptive distortions. Survivor bias occurs when managers are removed from the record because their results were unsatisfactory (or their fund was closed due to poor results). Deleting the poor performers artificially lifts or enhances the overall average, and investors who believe "figures don't lie" get deceived. In a related cause of bias, new mutual funds are "incubated" (to use the industry term) in groups for a few years. Then those with the best recent performance get presented to the public as new investment "opportunities." When these new funds are blended into the overall record with other funds, the calculated average performance again gets a lift—and investors again get deceived.

Caveat emptor. These biases can easily add as much as 100 basis points, or more, per annum. And the distortion produced by these two biases usually equals, and often exceeds, the apparent superiority of the selected managers. Meanwhile, advertising will tout the funds with the best records, so investors will hear most often from those that have been—so far—the most successful.

Moreover, as with any series of statistics, the starting point can be important. Many of the most impressive "gee whiz" charts of investment performance become quite ordinary by simply adding or subtracting one or two years at the start or the end of the period shown. Investors should always get the whole record—not just selected excerpts.

For users of performance measurement, a big problem is separating three very different factors that are often mixed together. One factor is the "sampling error"—the probability that the statistics do not equal the reality. As with any sample, there will be imprecision or uncertainty. In investment performance data, the sampling error is the degree to which the particular portfolio for the particular time period is not a fair and representative sample of the manager's work.

The second factor is the possibility that, during the measurement period, the market environment may have been favorable or unfavorable for the particular fund's way of investing. For example, funds of small cap stocks have had both very favorable and very unfavorable market environments during the past few decades. As a result, they all looked better than they really were in some years and looked worse than they really were in other periods.

The third factor is the skill—or *lack* of skill—of the manager. This is what many clients and managers most want to measure. But here's the rub: in the short run, sampling errors will usually have a much larger impact on the reported results than will the manager's skill. As noted earlier, it would take many decades of performance measurement to know whether the apparently superior results reflected the manager's *skill* or just good *luck*. By the time you gather enough data to determine whether your fund manager's results were due to skill or luck, it will be too late for a timely decision. (And at least one of you will probably have died of old age.)

The power of regression to the mean in investing is illuminated in Figure 16.1. Each row shows the returns achieved over the next three by investing with *last* year's first-, second-, third-, and fourth-quartile managers. Even a brief inspection of the data shows that the performance in each row is almost random. Past performance does *not* predict future performance.

Figure 16.1 Subsequent returns for managers

	Quartile rank in subsequent three years			
Alpha rank in base year	**First quartile**	**Second quartile**	**Third quartile**	**Fourth quartile**
First quartile	29.2%	16.2%	15.0%	20.6%
Second quartile	16.6	24.8	22.3	15.3
Third quartile	14.7	20.0	22.8	16.0
Fourth quartile	15.1	14.9	15.3	22.6

Take a careful look at the data in Figure 16.1. As you'll soon see, there's nothing *to* see. Net of fees, *there is no pattern*. Like Sherlock Holmes's dog that didn't bark, this lack of pattern *is* the pattern. As Gertrude Stein once said in dismissing the possibility of visiting Oakland, California, "There's no there there."

Most individual investors are aware of the ubiquitous ratings of mutual fund performance bestowed by investment research firm Morningstar. But Morningstar's one- to five-star ratings report only a fund's *past* performance. While the firm candidly says that its star ratings have little or no *predictive power*, 100 percent of the new investment money flowing into mutual funds goes to funds that were recently awarded four and five stars. (We've all seen the numerous ads trumpeting these high ratings.) This is too bad for investors because careful research concludes, "There is little statistical evidence that Morningstar's highest-rated funds outperform the medium-rated funds."[1] Indeed, in the months after the ratings are handed out each year, the five-star funds generally earn less than half as much as the broad market index! However unintentionally, Morningstar ratings are misleading investors into buying high and selling low.

The grievous lack of predictability of future performance on the basis of past performance is also shown in Figure 16.2, a stunning comparison of the results for the top 20 performers during a *bull* market and the results for the same funds in a *bear* market the very next year.[2]

Figure 16.2 Comparative fund performance in successive bull and bear markets

Rank in bull market*	Rank in bear market*
1	3,784
2	277
3	3,892
4	3,527
5	3,867
6	2,294
7	3,802
8	3,815
9	3,868
10	3,453
11	3,881
12	3,603
13	3,785
14	3,891
15	1,206
16	2,951
17	2,770
18	3,871
19	3,522
20	3,566

*Rank among 3,896 mutual funds in performance during the 12 months ended on March 30, 2000, and the 12 months ended on March 30, 2001.

Over very long periods, the average return obtained by most actively managed mutual funds must be expected to be close to the market average *minus* about 1.5 percent of costs each year for management fees, commissions on transactions, and custody expenses. (Given today's consensus expectation of 7 percent average annual returns, that 1.5 percent is over 20 percent of the expected returns. That is a very high cost.) So even if they are, before costs, slightly ahead of the market—thanks to all their hard work—most active managers can be expected to *lag* the market after fees and expenses (as is explained in Chapter 1). And this is what studies of investment performance consistently show (see Figure 16.3).

Figure 16.3 Long-term performance of mutual funds versus the market

Proportion of funds	Performance versus market
16%	−2% or worse
57	0 to -2%
26	0 to +2%
2	+2% or better

The dominant realities are clear: nearly three-quarters of active funds achieved *less* than market performance; only 2 percent of active funds were more than 2 percent ahead of the market over the whole period, and that's before taxes. (A much larger 16 percent were 2 percent or more *worse* than the market.) While understandable and even predictable, this record is not encouraging for investors who want to believe in active investing. And these data are favorably biased by "failed fund" deletions (as explained above).

If only 2 percent of mutual funds are significantly above the market and you share the view that the odds of finding the right two in a hundred are not good in a game played with real money, you would probably also agree that there is a fine alternative: index funds. In addition, as we've seen, income taxes are negligible with index funds because turnover is far lower and the funds can easily be managed to avoid incurring taxes.

Even more disconcerting for mutual fund investors, the average mutual fund investor actively gets a return that is significantly *below* the return of the average mutual fund he or she invests in.[3] From 1997 to 2011, the shortfall was stunning: investors got only one-half of the returns earned by the average equity mutual fund. Even investors in *bond* funds got less than their funds did. We've seen this movie before. A 1999 study concluded that while the S&P 500 gained an average of 17.9 percent a year over the 15 years from 1984 through 1998, the typical investor in stock funds gained only 7 percent a year over that same period.[4] The reason: frequent trading in and out of funds, chasing "performance." Instead of staying the course with their mutual funds, many investors tried to time the market cycles, typically holding a fund for less than three years before selling it and buying a different fund. When the income tax consequences of what has become typical portfolio turnover—60 percent or more annually—are deducted, mutual fund performance gets cut back even more.

The odds of outperforming the market get worse and worse—*and* more statistically significant—as the measurement period gets longer, as shown in Figure 16.4. One long-term study found that only 13.25 percent of surviving mutual funds beat the S&P 500. Note the qualifying term "surviving." As seen in Chapter 10, mutual fund companies bury their mistakes. So of all the funds that started out, the percentage that beat the market is even lower—much lower.

Figure 16.4 Very few mutual funds outperform the market over the long term

Period of time	Percentage of funds outperforming
1 year	35
10 years	20
25 years	10
50 years	5

A key concept is this: any unexpected and unexplained deviation from realistic expectation may signal poor performance. (A sensible proxy for realistic expectations of a mutual fund is the average performance of other funds with similar investment objectives.) A large unexplained deviation is very poor performance. And as every user of the statistical techniques for quality control[5] knows, it makes no qualitative difference whether the deviation is *above* or *below* expectation. Sure, we investors are trained to think that higher returns are better returns, and in the long run they certainly are. But in the shorter run, deviating above or below expectation indicates that the manager is out of conformance with his or her mission. And out of conformance usually means out of control—with unhappy results the probable eventual outcome. (A ship is just as far off course when it is 10 miles *west* of its objective as when it is 10 miles *east* of its objective.) It's nice for the investor to get a higher return than a lower return, but either one is off target, and the investor should not confuse good luck (or bad luck) with the manager's level of skill.

Information is data with a purpose. The purpose of measuring performance is to determine whether current portfolio operations are in faithful accord with long-term policy. Because performance measurement can be useful only when a valid standard has been clearly established, the usefulness of performance measurement depends on the clarity and specificity of the investor's investment policy.

A major problem for institutional investment managers and their clients is the dispersion in the performance of investment managers in the same organization or even by the same portfolio when managing portfolios with the same investment policies. The results should be the same, but the differences within a firm can and often are significant. For an investment organization, such dispersion indicates an important problem in internal quality control. Clients should request full disclosure of the results of *all* comparable portfolios managed by their portfolio manager and his or her firm.

One of the great frustrations professional investors have with short-term performance measurements is that bad decisions with favorable outcomes are often well received by amateur investors, while good decisions with temporarily unfavorable outcomes can lead to a loss of confidence—at just the wrong time. Investors who choose a mutual fund just after it has benefited from a particularly favorable market environment often impute to the fund manager a special set of skills and genius that will prove impossible to reproduce after that favorable market environment changes.

The final problem with performance measurement is its perverse tendency to stimulate counterproductive thinking and behavior by diverting the investor's interest and attention away from long-term policy and over to short-term operating results. The process of measuring almost certainly influences the phenomenon being measured, as the physicist Werner Heisenberg elucidated years ago with his principle of indeterminacy.

Sophisticated clients have been able to stay with investment managers who made good qualitative sense even when the quantitative measures of performance were disappointing—particularly when a manager was conscientiously and competently following his or her agreed-upon mandate even though that mandate happened to be temporarily out of tune with the market's current favorite sectors. In many cases, the subsequent performance has been rewarding to both manager and client. In fact, a good test of the care with which you have chosen a mutual fund would be this: if the fund underperformed the market because the manager's particular style was out of favor, would you cheerfully assign substantially *more* money to that fund? If your answer is yes, you recognize that the manager will almost certainly outperform the overall market averages when investment fashion again favors his or her style. This is the favorable side of regression to the mean, so why not take advantage of the opportunity?

Notes

1. C. R. Blake and M. R. Morey, "Morningstar Ratings and Mutual Fund Performance," *Journal of Financial and Quantitative Analysis*. 35, no. 3 (September 2000).
2. This "now you see it, now you don't" lack of meaning was first and most delightfully shown for individual common stocks years ago by Ian M. D. Little, the investment bursar of Nuffield College at Oxford, in his aptly titled essay "Higgledy Piggledy Growth."
3. Gary Belsky and Thomas Gilovich, *Why Smart People Make Big Money Mistakes* (New York: Simon & Schuster, 1999), 178.
4. Dalbar, Inc.
5. W. Edwards Deming and Joseph M. Juran built great careers helping manufacturers achieve superior product quality through such statistical techniques for analyzing consistency and conformance to plan and intention.

THE DARK MATTER
OF INVESTING

DARK FORCES HAVE BEEN STALKING ACTIVE INVESTMENT MAN-agement. Most insiders are understandably reluctant to recognize and discuss the real meaning of those forces, perhaps because they explain why active managers have, predictably, been more and more frequently failing. Most clients have not yet recognized that those powerful forces have been making it increasingly difficult for active managers to succeed in their self-chosen and self-celebrated mission: beating the market. The grim purpose of this chapter is to explain how much more disappointing investment performance has been than investment managers and selection consultants have reported.

Of course, some active managers will succeed over a decade. Fewer will succeed over longer runs. This dour reality is caused by two forces. First, as will be shown in Chapter 21, fees have increased, to surprisingly high levels when correctly calculated. Second, the huge influx of skillful, dedicated professionals with superb IT equipment and instant access to remarkably equal information has continued to reduce both the number of winners and the magnitude of their winning (*and* increase the number of managers unable to overcome the cost of their fees and their operations). As a result, the average practitioner today is much better equipped and more capable than his average predecessor. But so are his numerous competitors. Also, the distribution around the mean has become more and more concentrated. So it is much harder for any one manager to break out of the pack and achieve significantly better performance over the long run.

The important reality is that most actively managed mutual funds, in category after category, do not keep up with index funds with the same objectives. This crucial reality is shown dramatically in Figure 17.1, which is based on data from Morningstar, the trusted independent evaluator of mutual fund performance. The data in the following table are shown after the deduction of fees from all funds. Note particularly how low the "success rate" is over 10 years: not even half of the mutual funds in any category match or beat their chosen index or benchmark. In three out of four categories, less than 35 percent of the funds keep up with the standard they set out to beat. This grim reality is the crux of the matter for serious investors: overall, more than three out of four actively managed mutual funds are losers in the competition they themselves chose!

Figure 17.1 Active funds' low "success" rates by category

Category	1 Year	3 Years	5 Years	10 Years
Large Blend	27.7%	27.8%	16.3%	16.6%
Large Value	36.5	34.6	19.6	33.7
Large Growth	49.3	18.9	11.9	12.2
Small Blend	50.2	34.9	32.8	24.7
Small Value	66.7	54.1	38.0	38.3
Small Growth	22.3	28.6	20.6	23.2
Large Foreign	63.6	47.6	44.7	33.9
Emerging Markets	63.0	55.9	61.2	43.2

Source: Morningstar. Data and calculations as of December 31, 2015

At least as serious as the sizable shortfall, nearly half of the mutual funds *did not even survive* for the full 10 years. Those funds that were closed down (or merged into other, better-performing funds)—almost always for poor performance—were no less than:

- 48 percent of all large growth funds
- 47 percent of all small growth funds
- 40 percent of all large value funds
- 32 percent of all small value funds

These abandoned orphans are, of course, essential parts of the whole truth that all investors need to know and understand. Finally, Figure 17.2 shows the painful "sting in the tail" from funds that close, never again to be reported or even acknowledged. They typically declined sharply during their last 12 to 18 months.

Figure 17.2 How closed funds declined

Source: Vanguard calculations, using data from Morningstar, Inc.

Of course, most investors will not recognize such data. Most will say, "The performance numbers I've seen are *much* more favorable than these data. Something must be wrong!" What's wrong is this: the way numbers are selectively reported in advertisements and promotional materials gives investors a false—and much enhanced—impression of the performance of active managers. Alas, this deception is not accidental.

No law or regulation requires mutual fund organizations to keep reporting funds they no longer manage. Nor are they required to report how many funds in their family have been closed or merged into a stronger fund within the same family. Nor is there any requirement to continue reporting the poor performance that preceded the closure or merger. As a result, many mutual fund families do what their competitors do: in a race to the bottom, the poor and mediocre performers get quietly deleted from the database as though they had never existed. Adding the deleted failures back into the record converts soft, selective, "favorable" claims to hard, unfavorable evidence and flips the conclusion from "active usually works" over to "active usually does *not* work."

Similarly, when consultants that help institutional investors select investment managers drop a manager from their "recommended" list, they usually delete all past data on that manager. Why continue to report on a manager they no longer recommend? And when they *add* a new recommended manager, they add that manager's favorable results for prior years—retroactively. The result is a chart purporting to show that their chosen managers have outperformed. The data may be precise, but they are not accurate measures of the consultant's selection skills or record.

Given the many major changes in the composition of the securities markets, investors should recognize that it has been getting harder—much harder—for most active investment managers to outperform their chosen benchmarks. The data in Figure 17.3 include results for funds that were merged or closed—and confirm this pessimistic evaluation. In almost every category and in almost every year, active managers as a group underperform their own chosen benchmarks. The trend over time is for larger and larger percentages of active managers to *under*perform their benchmarks.

Figure 17.3 Percent of mutual funds failing to match their own benchmarks

Fund Category	Benchmark Index	2000	2001	2002	2003	2004	2005	2006	2007	2008	2009	2010	2011	2012	2013	2014	2015
All Domestic Funds	S&P Composite 1500	40.5	54.5	59.0	47.7	51.4	44.0	67.8	48.8	64.2	41.7	57.6	84.1	66.1	46.1	87.2	74.8
All Large Cap	S&P 500	36.9	57.6	61.0	64.6	61.6	44.5	69.1	44.8	54.3	50.8	61.8	81.3	63.3	55.8	86.4	66.1
All Mid Cap	S&P MidCap 400	78.9	67.3	70.3	56.4	61.8	76.0	46.7	46.4	74.7	57.6	78.2	67.4	80.5	39.0	66.2	56.8
All Small Cap	S&P SmallCap 600	70.7	66.4	73.6	38.8	85.0	60.5	63.6	45.0	83.8	32.2	36.0	85.8	66.5	68.1	72.9	72.2
Large Cap Growth	S&P 500 Growth	16.0	87.5	71.8	44.7	39.5	31.6	76.1	31.6	90.0	39.1	82.0	96.0	46.1	42.7	96.0	49.3
Large Cap Value	S&P 500 Value	54.5	20.6	39.4	78.5	8.32	58.8	87.7	46.3	22.1	46.2	34.7	54.3	85.0	66.6	78.6	59.1
Mid Cap Growth	S&P MidCap 400	78.4	79.0	87.0	31.7	59.7	78.6	34.9	39.3	89.0	59.7	82.1	75.4	87.2	36.7	56.2	79.9
Mid Cap Value	S&P MidCap 400 Value	94.8	55.8	74.3	81.9	63.6	71.8	38.4	56.1	67.1	47.8	71.8	64.9	76.2	45.3	73.6	32.4
Small Cap Growth	S&P SmallCap 600 Growth	73.0	81.3	94.2	35.3	93.6	72.2	52.1	39.4	95.5	33.5	72.7	93.8	63.7	55.6	64.5	88.4
Small Cap Value	S&P SmallCap 600 Value	74.4	48.7	37.5	49.3	77.5	46.0	77.0	39.9	72.5	26.3	51.8	83.0	61.8	79.0	94.3	46.6

Source: S&P Dow Jones Indices LLC, CRSP. Data as of December 31, 2015, based upon equal-weighted fund counts.

Data from Morningstar show a similar pattern of serious failures in category after category of equity mutual funds. In the 10 years ended in December 2015, 82 percent of large cap funds, 94 percent of large cap growth managers, 61 percent of large cap value managers, and 88 percent of small cap funds had results *below* their chosen benchmarks. At least as concerning, more than 40 percent of the 2,080 different funds that were tracked at one time during the past decade failed to perform and have been deleted, usually through termination or merger into a fund with a better record. Almost as concerning, only one out of three funds has sustained its original commitment to a particular investment style over the full 10 years.

Figure 17.4 shows that a full 40 percent of mutual funds were terminated within 10 years of their launch. In addition, only 36 percent of funds maintained the consistent style of investing they had promised to follow.

Figure 17.4 Survivorship and style consistency of equity funds over 10 years

Fund Category	Funds at Start	Survivorship	Style Consistency
All Domestic Funds	2110	60.0	35.9
All Large Cap Funds	672	56.4	39.1
All Mid Cap Funds	355	60.6	30.0
All Small Cap Funds	475	63.2	41.9
All Multi Cap Funds	608	61.9	31.4
Large Cap Growth Funds	204	49.0	35.3
Large Cap Value Funds	200	66.5	48.5
Mid Cap Growth Funds	171	51.5	32.8
Mid Cap Value Funds	89	73.3	20.9
Small Cap Growth Funds	184	54.9	44.6
Small Cap Value Funds	88	75.0	36.4

Source: S&P Dow Jones Indices LLC, CRSP. Data as of December 31, 2015.

"Caveat emptor" may be a conventional warning, but is that really sufficient? The deception of reporting significantly enhanced performance data—often to the second decimal, which *seems* to assure accuracy and precision—may be good for current sales, but it is hardly professionally responsible. If the mutual fund industry wants to continue to be trusted by millions of investors, doesn't it need to set higher standards for measuring and reporting investment performance?

CHAPTER 18

PREDICTING THE MARKET—ROUGHLY

INVESTORS NATURALLY WANT TO KNOW THE MOST PROBABLE investment outlook for the years ahead. Understanding the outlook for the next few days or weeks is easy. As J. P. Morgan famously said, "It will fluctuate." Long-term investors understand from experience the remarkable discipline of the bell curve of economic behavior and the central tendency of the major forces in the economy and the stock market to move toward "normal" via regression to the mean. One good way to be realistic about future returns is to assume that the future range of price/ earnings multiples and corporate profits will be within their historical upper and lower limits and will appear with increasing frequency at values closer and closer to the mean.

While the economy is extraordinarily complex at a detailed level—and the stock market reflects all sorts of factors in every domestic and global industry, in thousands of companies, and in the overall economy—two big factors dominate reality for investors: corporate profits (and the dividends they provide) and the price/earnings (P/E) ratio at which these earnings are capitalized. The price/earnings ratio is determined by interest rates, the outlook for profits and expected inflation, and an "equity premium" reflecting the uncertainty of investing in stocks, plus or minus a speculative factor reflecting how optimistic or pessimistic investors currently feel.

The best way to start a study of the future is to study the past. For the period 1901–1921, the inflation-adjusted average annual return of the U.S. stock market was just 0.2 percent. For the period 1929–1949, it was only 0.4 percent, and for 1966–1986, it was 1.9 percent. In other words, for periods covering more than 60 percent of the twentieth century, the real annual returns generated by the third-best-performing stock market in the world were less than 2.0 percent. And the first decade of the twenty-first century was worse. At year-end 1964 *and* at year-end 1981, the Dow Jones Industrial Average stood at 875—that's 17 long years with zero net change *before* adjusting for inflation. Even though corporate profits were up nicely, interest rates had soared from 4 percent to 15 percent, compressing the market's price/earnings multiple substantially. Investors had become deeply pessimistic.

From that low level, where did the market go? In 1988, dividends yielded 3.5 percent, and over the next 11 years earnings grew at an average of 7.1 percent annually. Good news for investors: the fundamental return of dividends plus earnings growth was 10.6 percent per annum. But that's not all—investors got paid a lot more. While the fundamental return was 10.6 percent, the total investment return was a stunning 18.9 percent. The difference was made up by the annual add-on of 8.3 percentage points in speculative return as the price/earnings ratio took flight and more than doubled from 12 to 29 at the millennium.

Could it last? Of course not. Regression to the mean was sure to come again. Just as a price/earnings multiple of 12 had been too low, a price/earnings multiple of 29 was too high and eventually sure to go down.

Historical perspective is always helpful.[1] How do these two major factors—earnings and P/E—explain America's best-ever bull market, from 1982 to 1999? Here's how: first, corporate profits in 1982 were only 3.5 percent of gross domestic product, significantly *below* the 4 to 6 percent normal range. By the late 1990s, corporate profits were almost 6 percent, the *high* side of the normal range. That's a big change. Next, interest rates on long-term U.S. government bonds plunged over that period from 14 percent to 5 percent. (This single change would multiply the market value of those bonds *eight*fold, or 13 percent compounded annually.) As with all long-term changes in the market's valuation, the main forces were fundamental and *objective*. Also included was an additional, *subjective* factor that depended on how investors felt: very pessimistic at the end of the bear market in the seventies and very optimistic in the late nineties. Over the same years—partly as a result of earnings growth but primarily because of the major decline in interest rates—as expectations for inflation fell substantially, the Dow (with all dividends reinvested) increased nearly *20* times, for a compounded annual return of 19 percent.

In cheerful disregard of the great powers driving regression to the mean, investors almost always project past market and economic behavior out into the future, somehow expecting more of the same. In the early 1970s, investors were sure that inflation would stay sky high and earnings would stay low or get even worse, and most newspapers and magazines featured the same grisly prospects. In 2000, investors were (almost predictably) overly optimistic, anticipating more of the same compounding. Investors who were particularly enamored of Internet stocks were chanting the mantra of all stock market bubbles: "This time it's different." (Past investor enthusiasms were canals in Britain in the 1830s, railroads in Europe and America in the 1850s, automobiles in the 1920s, and real estate in Japan in the 1980s.)

By 2007, the dot-com collapse had been forgotten and investors were again comfortable with above-average P/Es. Then the subprime mortgage debacle compounded into a cataclysmic "perfect storm" that slammed the markets down as credit markets froze, well-known banks and securities firms were suddenly closed, and fears of a major recession mushroomed. Once again, investors learned how difficult it is to estimate the near-term market.

To start, if dividends yield 1.5 percent and corporate earnings grow at 4.5 percent—the middle of their normal range of growth over the long term—then a composite of 6 percent is the reasonable first part of the fundamental rate of return to expect, before adjusting for inflation. Next, what change in valuation, if any, is reasonable? As a starting point, the average price/earnings ratio in recent decades has been about 15.5.

Benjamin Graham wisely cautioned in the introduction to his classic textbook *Security Analysis*: "Long-term investors must be careful not to learn too much from recent experience."[2] He was talking about the 1929 market crash and the ghastly months and years that followed. He could just as easily have been talking about the Internet market or the financial crisis of 2008–2009 or any of a long series of occasions when all or part of the stock market overreacted to recent events—sometimes positively and sometimes negatively—and short-term hopes or fears overwhelmed long-term valuations.

Predicting the stock market *roughly* is not hard, but predicting it accurately is truly impossible.[3] Equally, predicting approximately where the stock market will normally be in the long run is not hard, but even estimating how it will move over the next few months is nearly impossible—and pointless.

Notes

1. *Irrational Exuberance* (Princeton University Press, 2000), Robert Shiller's eloquent and fact-founded review of the U.S. stock market at the height of the "new economy" euphoria, is a superb example of a rational appraisal.
2. Benjamin Graham and David Dodd, *Security Analysis* (New York: McGraw-Hill, 1934 edition).

3. Forecasting the future is difficult—and not only because, as Yogi Berra once explained, "it doesn't last." In a study of over 80,000 forecasts by experts predicting changes in the past *rate* of change in their own fields of expertise, you could beat the experts by simply saying: one-third of the time, change will increase; one-third of the time, change will decrease; and one-third of the time, there will be no significant change in the rate of change.

CHAPTER 19

INDIVIDUAL INVESTORS

INDIVIDUAL INVESTORS ARE PROFOUNDLY DIFFERENT FROM INSTI-tutional investors like pension funds and endowments. It's not just that individual investors have less money. One difference is taxes. Active managers, with typically over 60 percent annual turnover, generate tax obligations that their investors must pay. So beware: declared investment performance is *before* taxes. Another difference is decisive: Every individual is mortal. And we all know, as individuals and as investors, that "life is short." While the exact timing is not known, mortality is a dominant reality for all individual investors.

Those of us who are earning incomes know we each have a finite number of years in which to build our savings for retirement security. And those who are no longer earning and saving have finite financial resources, on which they will depend for the indefinite duration of their lives.

While the key to success in investing is *rationality*, most investors can't help letting their emotions get involved and, at certain market junctures, even get the upper hand. Individual investors' money often takes on great symbolic meaning and can engage investors' emotions powerfully—all too often, too powerfully. Many investors feel that their money represents them and the worth of their lives (just as entrepreneurs often identify their self-worth with their companies). This "my money is me" syndrome is particularly common among elderly people and can cause irascible or even petty behavior. (If it happens to someone in your family, be tolerant: It's probably just another way of expressing fear of death.)

Yet another important reality is that individual investors have considerable power to affect others—both financially and emotionally—with gifts and bequests made or not made, made larger or smaller than anticipated, or considered fair or unfair. Within a family, the emotional power and symbolism of money are often more important than its economic power. Individual investors will be wise to deal carefully with both.

Individual investors, as we know, usually buy stocks for reasons *outside* the stock market. They buy because they inherit money, get a bonus, sell a house, or for any other happy reason have money to invest as a result of something that has no direct connection to the stock market. Similarly, they sell stocks because a child is going off to college or they have decided to buy a home—almost always for reasons *outside* the stock market.

Unlike the full-time professionals who so completely dominate today's stock markets, individual investors typically do not do extensive, rigorous comparison shopping across the many alternatives within the stock market. Most individual investors are not experts on even a few companies. Individuals may *think* they know something important when they invest, but almost always what they think they know is either not true or not relevant or not important new information. The amateur's "scoop" is usually already well known and factored into the market price by the professionals who are active in the market all the time. Thus, the activity of most individual investors is what market researchers correctly call "informationless" trading or "noise." (These terms are not meant to be rude; they are simply descriptive. Anyone who feels offended by them is being too sensitive.)

It is little wonder that way back in the 1960s the pioneers of professional investing were working *inside* the market, making rigorous and well-informed comparisons of price to value across hundreds and hundreds of different stocks on which they could command up-to-the-minute information—and that they were confident they could outperform the individual amateur investors who did 90 percent of the trading. Back then, the professionals could and did outperform the amateurs' market. But that was half a century ago.

Now the picture is profoundly different. After 50 years of enormous growth in mutual funds, pension funds, and hedge funds *and* increasing turnover in those institutions' portfolios, the old 90:10 ratio has been completely reversed. Today 99 percent of all New York Stock Exchange trades are made by investment professionals. In fact, 75 percent of all trading is done by the professionals at the 100 largest and most active institutions, and fully half of all NYSE trading is done by the professionals at just the 50 largest and most active institutional investors.

Just how tough to beat are the 100 largest institutions? Here are some realities: The very largest institutions each pay their leading stockbrokers as much as $100 million *apiece*. The stockbrokers earn it by making the best markets and providing the best research services they can deliver. The institutions have multiple Bloomberg terminals and all the other extensive information services *and* powerful computers with sophisticated models and programs. They all have teams of in-house analysts and senior portfolio managers with an average of 20-plus years of investing experience—all working their contacts and networks to get the best information all the time. You get the picture: compared with an individual investor, the institutional investor has all the advantages.

All investors share one all too easily underestimated risk: inflation. This adversary can be dangerous for individual investors—and most particularly dangerous for retired people—as it certainly was in the seventies. Because we now have so little inflation, many assume it will never come again. The Federal Reserve target is now 2 percent inflation, but perfect control is not likely and 3 or 4 percent inflation is certainly possible.

Over the long run, inflation has been a major problem for investors, more serious than the attention-getting daily or cyclical changes in securities prices that most investors fret about. The corrosive power of inflation can be truly daunting: at 2 percent "normal" inflation, the purchasing power of money is cut in half in 36 years (see Figure 19.1). At 5 percent inflation, the purchasing power of your money is cut in half in just 14 years, and it gets cut in half *again* in the next 14 years to just one-quarter. In our society, the average person can expect to live to about 86. When you are retired and have no way to offset the dreadful erosion of purchasing power caused by inflation, this is clearly serious business.

Figure 19.1 Effect of increasing inflation on purchasing power

Rate of inflation (%)	Years to cut your money in half
2	36
3	24
4	18
5	14
6	12

Individual investors have responsibilities they take personally: educating children, providing a good family home, providing security in retirement, providing a strong self-defense against catastrophe or the risk of living longer and needing more healthcare than anticipated, helping to pay for healthcare for elderly relatives, contributing to the schools and other institutions from which they have benefited or hope their communities will benefit, and more. Finally, most individuals wish to leave something to their children or grandchildren to enhance *their* lives. (Children having better lives than their parents and grandparents is, for most people, the real meaning of progress.) For some needs, particularly healthcare late in life, the amount of money that will be required is unknown and may become almost unlimited.

In planning the responsibility side of your "total financial picture" balance sheet, you'll want to decide who is included in your "we"—and for what purpose. Doing so will be useful and informative. How much responsibility do you plan to take for your children's education? College is costly. Graduate school is increasingly accepted as the norm, and it's costly too. After providing for education, is helping with a child's first home important to you? Help in starting a business or a dental practice? How about your parents, brothers and sisters, or your in-laws? Under what circumstances would they need your financial help? How much might be involved, and when? Be sure you know what your total commitments might add up to and when the money might be needed, so you can plan ahead.

Because we can invest only what we have saved, saving necessarily comes before investing. Saving has one special characteristic: you can decide what you want done, and you can *make* it happen! Buying straw hats in the fall or Christmas cards in January, driving a "preowned" car, and owning a smaller house than you could afford all count as saving. Many other daily forms of conscientious underspending can make a splendid difference over the years, particularly when matched with a sensible long-term approach to investing. One powerful way to save is to limit your spending to *last* year's income. And always be sure to "max out" contributions to your tax-sheltered retirement fund.

The first purpose of saving is to accumulate a defensive reserve that, like a fire extinguisher, can be used when trouble comes. And like a fire extinguisher, such a reserve should be used boldly and fully whenever needed. The reserve is on hand to be *spent*. If you use your defensive reserve cautiously or only partially, you will simply require a proportionately larger reserve. It is expensive in opportunity costs to have a larger reserve than is really needed. After providing for protection against serious contingencies, invest for the long term.

A core concept of this book is that funds available for long-term investment will do best for the investor if they are invested in stocks and kept in stocks over the long term. This guideline is particularly important for young working investors, for two major reasons. First, even at 7 percent returns, every dollar saved and invested will be two dollars in 10 years, four dollars in 20 years, eight dollars in 30 years, and so on and so on—following the Rule of 72.[1] Second, taking a total view of your financial picture, your largest "asset" is your ability to earn income year after year, probably in increasing amounts. This earning power can be viewed much like a bond and in the individual's twenties, thirties, and even forties will be a large percentage of the total financial picture (see Chapter 13).

But what about elderly investors whose life expectancy is less than the 10 years that usually approximate "long term"? Shouldn't they, as the conventional wisdom would have it, invest primarily in bonds to preserve capital? As usual, the conventional wisdom *may* be wrong. While retired investors may decide, for peace of mind, that they prefer to invest in relatively stable securities with relatively high income, they may be letting their emotional interests dominate their economic interests.

While elderly investors may not expect to live for many more years, their investments, after being inherited by beneficiaries, may have a very long-term mission. Why limit the time horizon for thinking about investments to the owner's lifetime when the owner's true objectives—providing for children, grandchildren, or alma mater—have a much longer-term horizon? Besides, one of the secrets to a long and happy life is to keep climbing and stay, in Disraeli's felicitous phrase, "in league with the future." Investing in stocks can help keep us thinking young.

To be a truly successful lifetime investor, the first and central challenge is to know thyself—to understand your personal financial goals and what would truly be successful for *you*. Remember the wise counsel of author Adam Smith: "If you don't know who you are, the stock market is an expensive place to find out." So are the markets for real estate, commodities, and options. Investors will be wise to take time to learn as much as possible about themselves—and how they will feel and behave as investors during market highs and lows. We need to know our true selves so we can put our best rational thinking in control of our own emotions. For example, here's a simple test—with a friendly twist.

Question: If you had your choice, which would you prefer?

Choice A: Stocks go *up*—by quite a lot—and *stay up* for several years.
Choice B: Stocks go *down*—by quite a lot—and *stay down* for several years.

Make your choice *before* you look at the next paragraph.

Without looking ahead, which did you choose? If you selected choice A, you would be joining 90 percent of the investors—both individual and professional—who've taken this test. Comforted to know that most investors agree with you? You shouldn't be. Unless you are a *seller* of stocks, you would have chosen *against* your own interests if you chose A.

Here's why: First, remember that when you buy a common stock, what you really buy is the right to receive the dividends paid on that share of stock.[2] Just as we buy cows for their milk and hens for their eggs, we buy stocks for their current and future earnings and dividends. If you ran a dairy, wouldn't you prefer to have cow prices low when you were buying so you could get more gallons of milk for your investment in cows?

The lower the price of the shares when you buy, the more shares you will get for every $1,000 you invest and the greater the dollars you will receive in future dividends as a percentage of your investment. Therefore, if you are a saver and a buyer of shares, as most investors are and will continue to be for many years, your real long-term interest is, curiously, to have stock prices go *down* quite a lot and stay down. That's why you can accumulate more shares at low prices and so receive more future dividends with the money you invest. So the right long-term choice is counterintuitive choice B.

I hope this insight will enable you to enjoy greater success as an investor *and* greater peace of mind during the inevitable bear markets during your investing career. (You may even learn to see a benefit in bear markets. If you're really rational, you will.)

Most investors, being all too human, much prefer stock markets that have been rising and feel most enthusiastic about buying more shares when stock prices are already high, axiomatically causing the future rate of return from their dividends to be low *and* their risk of market losses high. Similarly, most investors feel quite negative about stocks *after* share prices have gone down and are most tempted to sell out at the really wrong time—when prices are already low *and* the future dividend yield on the price paid will be high (see Figure 19.2). As shown in the chart, a 1927 dollar grew to $106 over 72 years as a result of price appreciation.

Figure 19.2 Reinvesting dividends has been important

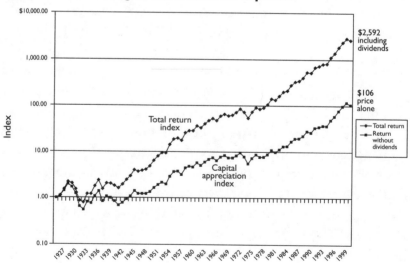

In my first year on Wall Street, over 50 years ago, I was in a training program with a group of freshly minted MBAs. We all looked forward to our final session, a meeting with the senior partner, a patrician who had amassed a major fortune through astute investing over many years.[3] Asked about his secret for success and what he would advise young men like us to do, he took a long, thoughtful pause and then summarized his accumulated experience in this short maxim: "Don't lose!"

When first heard, his advice seemed simplistic. But as the years have gone by, I've become convinced that the advice was and is very sound. Naturally, you can't invest without absorbing lots of small interim losses because markets do fluctuate, but don't risk serious, irrevocable losses. Don't invest with borrowed money. As mentioned earlier, there are no old, bold pilots.

If you find yourself getting caught up in the excitement of a rising market or distressed by a falling market, stop. Go for a walk and cool down. Otherwise, you will soon become part of the crowd, wanting to *do* something—and you will start making mistakes, perhaps grave mistakes that you will later regret. Benign neglect is, for most investors, the secret to long-term success in investing.

If you have successfully saved and invested enough to have ample funds for all your chosen responsibilities and obligations, you have truly *won* the money game. Bravo! This is an appropriately thrilling achievement.

Winners should be careful, however, never to put their victory at risk in an attempt to win *big*, particularly through unnecessarily borrowing, committing too much to any single investment, or overextending responsibilities and commitments. Winners should also avoid speculating. It's not worth the risk of becoming a big loser—truly a sucker. Winners should be equally careful about being too careful.

For an individual investor, these 10 "commandments" may be useful guides to thinking about your decisions on investments:

1. Save. Invest your savings in your future happiness and security, education for your kids, and fiscal freedom to choose.

2. If you must "play the market" to satisfy an emotional itch, recognize that you are gambling on your ability to beat the pros. So limit the amounts you play with to the same amounts you would set aside to gamble with the pros in Las Vegas. (Keep accurate records of your results, and you'll soon persuade yourself to quit!)

3. Don't do anything in investing primarily for tax reasons. Tax shelters are usually poor investments. Tax-loss selling is primarily a way for brokers to increase their commissions. (There are exceptions. Be sure you have an astute estate plan that is current with your financial situation and the ever-changing tax laws. Making charitable gifts of low-cost stock that has appreciated in value can make sense *if* you were going to sell the stock anyway. Set up an IRA if you can, and maximize contributions to your tax-sheltered 401(k) or profit-sharing plan every year. If you have investments outside your 401(k), make your investment decisions based on your total picture: To minimize income taxes, any bonds or bond funds belong in your tax-sheltered retirement fund.)

4. Don't think of your home as an investment. Think of it as a store of value and a nice place to live with your family—period. A home is not a good financial

(Continued)

good, but not invest.

investment and never was. But a home can certainly be a fine investment in your family's happiness. House prices will always center on the cost to replace an existing home with a new one. Due to increasing efficiency in construction, after adjusting for inflation the cost of building a new home is about the same as 50 years ago.

5. Don't do commodities.[4] Dealing in commodities is really only price speculation. It's not investing because there's no economic productivity or value added.

6. Don't get confused about stockbrokers and mutual fund salespeople. They are usually very nice people, but their job is not to make money *for* you. Their job is to make money *from* you. While a few stockbrokers are wonderfully conscientious people devoted to doing a thoughtful job for the customers they work with over many, many years, you can't assume that your stockbroker is working that way for you. Some do, but most simply can't afford it. Be realistic. The typical stockbroker "talks to" 200 customers with *total* invested assets of $5 million. To earn $100,000 a year, he or she needs to generate about $300,000 in gross commissions, or 6 percent of the money he or she talks to. To generate this volume of commissions—heavy expenses to the investors—the broker cannot afford the time to learn what is "right." He or she has to keep the money—*your* money—moving.

mrkt pros not friend

7. Don't invest in new, interesting kinds of investments. They are all too often designed to be *sold to* investors, not to be *owned by* investors. (When the novice fisherman expressed wonderment that fish would actually go for the gaudily decorated lures offered at the bait

(Continued)

shop, the proprietor's laconic reply was, "We don't sell them lures to fish.")

8. Don't invest in bonds just because you've heard that bonds are conservative or for safety. Bond prices fluctuate, and bonds are a poor defense against the major risk of long-term investing: inflation.

9. Write out your long-term goals, your long-term investing program, and your estate plan—and then stay with them. While annual reviews of your investments are recommended, review your estate plans at least once each decade.

10. Distrust your feelings. When you feel euphoric, you're probably in for a bruising. When you feel glum, remember that it's darkest just before dawn, so take no action. Activity in investing is almost always in surplus supply. Less *is* better.

Finally, here is a special word to those who participate in a 401(k) plan—or any other "defined contribution" plan over which you, as a participant, have investment discretion. Concentrate on index funds. Do *not* invest in your own company, wonderful as the company may be, because income from that one company is already a major concentration in your total economic portfolio. Your retirement fund should be organized for safety first, and safety means *defense*. If you have any doubts, read all about Polaroid and Enron—two of the numerous major U.S. companies that later lost all their market value, obliterating many employees' retirement savings, *and* were forced to lay off large numbers of loyal workers. Result: retirement savings lost, jobs lost, and dreams lost.

Notes

1. The Rule of 72 tells how long a rate of increase takes to double the initial amount (or vice versa). For example, at 10 percent, the initial amount doubles in 7.2 years, and at 15 percent it takes 4.8 years; at 3 percent it takes 24 years.

2. Yes, you also get the right to vote on the selection of auditors, the election of directors, and so forth. And you get the right to be bought out at a higher price if and when there's a future takeover. But realistically, few votes of shareholders go against management's recommendations, and unanticipated buyouts occur at few companies. So these shareholder rights are usually not very important compared with dividends. Yes, you also get the right to sell the stock to another investor, hopefully at a higher price. But what determines the price the next investor will gladly pay? The present value of expected future earnings and dividends.

3. Joseph K. Klingenstein of Wertheim & Co.

4. John Train, *The Money Masters* (New York: Harper & Row, 1987) tells the full story. Consider the experience of a commodities broker who over a decade advised nearly 1,000 customers on commodities. How many made money? Not even one. But the broker did, thanks to commissions.

CHAPTER 20

SELECTING MUTUAL FUNDS

IF YOU ARE UNABLE OR UNWILLING TO ACCEPT INDEXING YET, YOU have two alternatives: You can make your own investment decisions, or you can invest in actively managed mutual funds. If, after reading this short book, you still decide to pick your own stocks, please do yourself a favor and keep a careful record of your decisions, what you expected when you made each one, how they worked out, and all the costs.

Stockbrokers may say that you pay nothing for their investment advice, their firm's research, or all the services you get. But take time to record all the costs, and you'll soon find that the stockbrokerage commissions you're paying can easily add up over a year's time to a much higher total cost as a percentage of your assets than the fees of a mutual fund.

Investing is *not* a hobby. Every major study has found that average results for self-reliant individual investors are poor. Moreover, the dispersion of results above and below that average is quite wide, so all too many investors get stuck with *very* poor results. That's why stockbrokers typically lose more than 20 percent of their customers every year. And almost all those customers lost real money—money they can never win back.

Start by knowing what your own investment objectives and staying power really are. Determining your investment staying power will help you set the level of market risk you can and will live with. Don't overcommit. Know your internal sensitivity to market risk and stay within your own limitations. As my father wisely advised, "Never risk more than you know you can afford to lose."[1]

Study your own record of decisions over the years to see how well *you* perform as an investor, and examine your capacity to tolerate market adversity in different time frames. It's one thing to know your ability to handle quarter-to-quarter fluctuations; they are usually relatively modest and soon reversed. It's another thing to absorb and accept a full bear market, particularly one that lasts longer and plummets more than normal. For example, ask: How did you feel when stocks lost over 45 percent of their value in 2008? How did you feel *and* how did you act under the ferocious pressures as day after day the market fell again and again?

Past performance records do not predict future results. Cambridge Associates, a firm that advises endowments, reports candidly, "There is no sound basis for hiring or firing managers solely on the basis of recent performance." In fact, if you divide all managers into deciles based on their past results, the data have almost zero predictive power. The one exception: the worst losers do tend to keep losing.

You may still want to select your own mutual funds, so here's a suggestion: You can jump-start your search by getting a list of the leaders in 401(k)s or other defined contribution plans from *Money, Forbes,* or *Bloomberg Businessweek.* Then ask your most knowledgeable acquaintances which of these funds consistently attract the best people and are most likely to achieve good results over the very long term. Your list will soon be dominated by such outstanding organizations as American Funds (managed by Capital Group Companies), T. Rowe Price, Wellington, and Vanguard.[2] Look for organizations that charge low fees and whose professionals invest most of their own net worth in their employers' own funds.

When selecting an actively managed mutual fund, make your selection in a deliberately unorthodox way. Do *not* pick one fund. Instead, start with a "ballpark" decision. Rather than trying to find *the* best mutual fund, look for a superior investment organization that offers a full family of mutual funds. Ask around. Is that organization considered a great place to work that consistently attracts and keeps first-rate people? Does it manage itself primarily as a *professional* organization rather than a *commercial* organization? The key to investment success is not found in the last few years' performance numbers; it's in the long-term professional culture of the organization.

Stocks and investment ideas come and go; fund managers come and go; but character in a person or culture in an organization—good or bad—is hard to change. So look for the culture that attracts and keeps superior people for 30- or 40-year careers. Look for consistency in statements about "how we do things here." And be wary and skeptical of organizations that try to get you to focus on recent results when your true interests are all long term. Eventually, character or organizational culture will surely dominate. So look for a well-established organization with a good long-term record, an organization that is respected and admired by knowledgeable investment people and will be comfortable to live with over the long term.

The idea of "comfortable to live with" is the key to long-term investment success for most individuals investing in mutual funds, because you do not want to change funds. Change is the investor's enemy in two ways. First, the cost of changing mutual funds may *look* small—switching funds "only costs a few percent" of assets—but all too many of those who change funds do so every few years, and those costs of change keep adding up. Second, most investors who change funds pay much larger, but hidden, costs because they sell after the worst part of the losses and buy after the best part of the gains. Watch the total industry money flows: most of the selling comes *after* a fund has already underperformed, and most of the buying comes *after* a fund has already outperformed. And the inflows and outflows are largest for the funds with the most dramatic ups and downs. So the self-inflicted pain is all the worse.

Sales-driven mutual fund companies may look back with understandable pride at how very far they've come as entrepreneurial businesses. But all too few recognize that in winning the confidence of more than 100 million individuals and over half of the families in the United States, mutual fund companies have not only won the battle for business success, they have also transformed themselves from *business* organizations into organizations with large fiduciary responsibilities because they have accepted the public trust. So whether the companies recognize it or not, the standards are now very different.

How many different mutual funds should you use? Not many! With mutual funds, an investor usually can find several different styles or classes of investing offered by any one major family of funds: index funds of different kinds, growth funds versus value funds, large cap versus small cap, money market funds, real estate investment trusts (REITs), international versus global, and many more. All the funds offered by a well-managed family of funds will be organizationally accountable for the same standards of professionalism, reasonable fees, and investor service. That's why it makes sense to choose carefully and concentrate your mutual fund investing with one fund family whose long-term investment results, business values, and practices you respect.

Wise investors choose mutual funds carefully and then stay the course. A good rule that is simple to state but very difficult for most investors to follow is this: never choose a mutual fund you would not confidently "double up" on if the fund's performance was significantly behind the market for two or three years *and* popular opinion was that the fund's manager had somehow lost his or her touch. Most mutual funds with superior long-term performance success have, within their long-term record, three straight years of subpar performance. So strive to keep faith with a steady, long-term program and ignore Mr. Market's shenanigans.

You know from personal experience at ticket counters and airport security lines that it usually does not pay to switch from one line to another.[3] Switching investment managers is even less productive, and switching funds is costly. Staying with a competent mutual fund manager who is conforming to his or her own promises—particularly when he or she is out of phase with the current market environment—shows real "client prudence" in investing and ultimately will be rewarded.

Because the easy answer is to use index funds, be sure any decision to pay up for an actively managed fund is the right decision for you. Many major changes have collectively transformed investing so much that most investors will find most actively managed mutual funds have not and cannot keep up with the market.

Rare is the mutual fund that achieves long-term results substantially superior *after* adjustment for risk. The data are as grim as a photograph of the 1913 graduating class of Saint-Cyr, France's military academy, destined for combat in the trenches of World War I. For over 50 years, mutual funds in the aggregate lost 180 basis points compounded annually to the S&P 500, returning 11.8 percent versus 13.6 percent for the benchmark index.[4] Over the past two decades, index fund returns have exceeded the results of more than 80 percent of all U.S. mutual funds. After years of careful study, Princeton's popular professor Burt Malkiel has found that the best estimate of a mutual fund's future performance relative to other mutual funds is based on just two factors: portfolio turnover and expenses. In both cases, less is more.

Notes

1. In the mid-1970s, I made a major commitment to John Neff's Gemini Fund. I knew John well enough to know that he was unusually careful to control and limit risk—while conventional investors were not discriminating carefully between real risk and perception, John clearly did. The stock market was in the depths of a major bear market and had been particularly negative on the value stocks John liked to own. As a closed-end dual-purpose fund—with one class of shares getting all the dividend income and a second class getting all the capital gains—Gemini's Capital shares had experienced the adverse leveraged impact of a multiyear, major decline in the stock market *and* were selling at a large discount from net asset value. I calculated how much broker's margin could be used without getting a margin call, even after a further 20 percent drop in stock prices, and bought in, fully margined. As the market rose, I enjoyed six layers of benefits: John Neff as my investment manager, plus the recovery of the market, plus the superior returns to value stocks, plus the shift from "discount" to "premium" in the Gemini Capital shares, plus the leverage of the duo-fund, plus the leverage of heavy margin. Despite all the apparent leverage risk, I felt very confident and quite safe for one great reason: I knew that John was both rigorously risk-averse and a disciplined, rational investor. The following 10 years, thanks to John's great work as the professional investor's favorite investment professional, were very well rewarded.

2. Full disclosure: I've written a book celebrating Capital Group and was a director of Vanguard for many years, and consulted on strategy for decades with T. Rowe Price and Wellington.

3. This phenomenon is called Ettore's Law.

4. John C. Bogle, "The Clash of Cultures in Investing: Complexity Versus Simplicity," speech given at the Money Show, Orlando, Florida, February 3, 1999.

CHAPTER 21

PHOOEY ON PHEES![1]

THE PRICING OF INVESTMENT MANAGEMENT SERVICES HAS BEEN an exception to the hallowed laws of economics for the past 50 years. Interestingly, this exception is a status most contemporary buyers and sellers of investment services appear to assume will continue forever—but may now be subject to change, even to substantial disruption.

Though some critics grouse about them, most investors have long thought investment management fees are best described with one three-letter word: low. In particular, fees are seen as so low that they are almost inconsequential when choosing an investment manager.[2]

This view of fees is a delusion of investors—and a not-so-innocent deception by investment managers. Framing, the way we describe and see something, can make a major difference. And so it has been with investment management fees. Seen correctly for what they really are, fees for active management are very high—and much higher than even most critics of fees have recognized.

When stated as a percentage of *assets*, average fees do look low: a little over 1 percent of assets for individuals[3] and a little less than one-half of 1 percent for institutional investors. But is this the right way to measure or describe fees? No! Not even close!

fees should be measured [illegible] results [illegible] not assets under mngt

Here's why. The investors already have their assets, so investment management fees should really be based on what investors are getting and what managers are expected to produce: returns.

Calculated correctly as a percentage of *returns*, fees no longer look low. Do the math. If future stock returns average, as most observers seem to expect, 7 percent a year, then those same fees are not 1 percent or 0.5 percent. They are much higher: more than 14 percent for individuals and over 7 percent for institutions.

But even this recalculation substantially understates the real cost of active investment management. That's because index funds produce a "commodity product" that reliably delivers the market rate of return with no more than market risk. Index funds are now available at fees that are very small: 0.10 percent or less for individuals and 0.03 percent or even less for institutions.

Because the commodity product is available to all investors, we should apply the lesson learned in Economics 101: When a reliable commodity product is widely available, the real cost of any alternative is the *incremental* cost as a percentage of the *incremental* value. So rational investors should consider the true cost of fees charged by active managers not as a percentage of total returns but as the *incremental* fee as a percentage of risk-adjusted *incremental* returns above the market index. Thus, correctly stated, management fees for active management are remarkably *high*.[4]

If you think that the level of fees should be in proportion to the actual benefit the fund shareholder gets, you'll be impressed to learn that the fees most mutual funds charge, relative to incremental risk-adjusted returns, are *over* 100 percent. That's right: *All* the value added over the index commodity product—plus some—goes to the fund manager. And there's nothing left over for the investors who put up all the money and took all the risk. It *is* a funny business—and worth thinking about. Are any other services of any kind priced at such a high proportion of client-delivered value? How long can active investment managers continue to thrive on the assumption that clients won't figure out the reality that, compared with the readily available index fund alternative, fees for active management are astonishingly high?

Fees for active management have a long and interesting history. Once upon a time—50 years ago—investment management was considered a loss leader. When pension funds mushroomed as "fringe benefits" during the post–World War II wage-and-price freeze, major banks controlled most of this new business by agreeing to manage pension fund assets as a "customer accommodation" for little or no *explicit* fee.

But they found a backdoor way to "monetize" their activities. With the high, fixed-rate brokerage commissions of those days, the banks exchanged trust department brokerage commissions for the large cash balances arising from retail customers' accounts. Under the terms of these agreements, brokers got "reciprocal" commission business (averaging about 40 cents per share) and, in exchange, the banks got large, idle cash balances in customers' accounts that they could lend out at prevailing interest rates. Both parties benefited—but not the brokers' customers, whose money was the "mother's milk" in the silent arrangement.

In the sixties, a few institutional brokerage firms, like Donaldson, Lufkin & Jenrette; Mitchell Hutchins; and Baker Weeks, had investment management units that nominally charged full fees (usually 1 percent) but then offset those nominal fees entirely by deducting the brokerage commissions generated by their active management practices—so their real fees were actually *zero*.

The new managers found that they could easily charge much more than banks and insurance companies because higher fees were seen as a confirmation of their expected superior performance. Compared with the magnitude of the predicted superior performance, the fees for active investment simply did not seem to matter. Any quibbling about fees was easily dismissed with comments like, "You wouldn't choose your child's brain surgeon on the basis of price, would you?"[5]

When the Morgan Bank took the lead in the late sixties by announcing it would charge institutional fees of one-quarter of 1 percent,[6] conventional Wall Street wisdom held that the move would cost the bank a ton of business. Clients would never accept such a high charge! Actually, Morgan lost only one small account. So managers realized that fees could be raised—and they were.

Thus began nearly a half century of persistent fee increases, facilitated by client perceptions that fees would be comfortably exceeded by incremental returns if the right managers were chosen. Even today, despite extensive evidence to the contrary, both individual and institutional investors somehow expect *their* chosen managers to produce significantly higher-than-market returns. That's apparently why fees have seemed low.

Decade after decade, assets of mutual funds and pension funds multiplied, and at the same time, fee schedules for active investment management tripled or quadrupled—instead of going down, as might be expected. With this combination, the investment business grew increasingly profitable. High pay and interesting work attracted rising numbers of highly capable MBAs, MDs, and PhDs to become analysts and portfolio managers *and*, collectively, more competition for one another.

Estimates of the number of professionals now devoted to various aspects of "price discovery" range from 500,000 to 1 million—up from perhaps 5,000 fifty years ago. Meanwhile, particularly during the high returns of the great bull market of the last quarter of the twentieth century, investors continued to ignore fees because almost everyone assumed that fees were unimportant.[6] Fees for investment management are remarkable in a significant way: nobody actually pays the fees by writing a check for an explicit amount. Instead, fees are quietly and automatically deducted by the investment managers and by custom are stated not in dollars, but as a percentage of assets.

Now, with return experience and return expectations both lower, a previously overlooked reality is getting more attention:

while asset-based fees have increased substantially over the past 50 years—more than fourfold for both institutional and individual investors—investment results have *not* improved, as a result of many major, compounding changes in the stock markets of the world, particularly the massive influx of skillful competitors.

If the upward trend of fees and the downward trend of prospects for "beat the market" performance wave a warning flag for investors—as they most certainly should—objective reality should cause all investors who think investment management fees are low to reconsider.[7] Seen in the right perspective, we now know, active management fees are *not* low. Fees are *high*—very high.

Over the past 50 years, trading volume has increased 1,000 times—from 4 million shares a day to 4 billion—while derivatives, in value traded, have risen from zero to more than the cash market. Institutional activity on the stock exchanges has gone from under 10 percent of trading to over 98 percent. And game changers such as the proliferation of Bloomberg terminals, CFAs, computer models, the Internet's globalization of information, hedge funds, high-frequency trading, activist investors, acquisitive corporations, and large private equity funds have all become major factors in the market.

More important, the worldwide increase in the number of highly trained professionals, all working intensively to achieve *any* competitive advantage, has been phenomenal. So today's stock market prices are an aggregation of all the expert estimates of price-to-value coming every day from extraordinary numbers of hardworking, independent, experienced, well-informed professional decision makers. The result is the world's largest-ever "prediction market." Against this consensus of experts, managers of diversified portfolios of publicly traded securities who strive to beat the market with high portfolio turnover are deeply challenged.

The SEC's Reg FD—Regulation Fair Disclosure—requires all listed companies to make sure that all information of any investment value is simultaneously made available to *all* investors.

What was the "secret sauce" of active managers in the last century is now a universal commodity. Almost everybody has almost all of what almost anybody has. So all are equal now.

Extensive, undeniable data show how exceedingly difficult it is for anyone to identify in advance any particular investment manager who will—after costs, taxes, and the fees now charged—achieve that holy grail of beating the market. Yes, Virginia, some managers will always beat the market, but we have no reliable way of determining in advance which specific managers will be the lucky ones.

Price is surely not everything, but just as surely, when analyzed as incremental fees for incremental returns, investment management fees are now very large. No wonder increasing numbers of individual and institutional investors are turning to index funds and ETFs and those with experience with either or both are steadily increasing their use.

Their reasoning is well worth careful consideration: First, most active management does not win for clients because so much "talent congestion" makes it a loser's game that is not worth playing. Second, the exceptional managers who will beat the market are too hard to separate in advance from managers who *appear* to be exceptional. Third, why not accept the persistent good performance of indexing and pay less in fees and taxes?

For those who already do index, active management appears to be another example of the triumph of hope over experience. Can active investment managers continue to thrive on the assumption that clients won't figure out the reality that, compared with the readily available indexing alternative, fees for active management are astonishingly high?

One thing is clear: few, if any, indexers would consider switching from indexing to active management. Why pay over 10 times the fees (plus more in taxes) to get more uncertainty *and* lower long-term returns *plus* the risk of a serious and costly manager disappointment?

Meanwhile, those hardworking and happy souls immersed in the fascinating complexities of active investment management might wonder: Is industrywide compensation for active management now in a global bubble of its own creation? Does a specter of declining fees haunt the industry's future?

Notes

1. The title of this chapter comes from Charlotte Beyer via her fine book *Wealth Management Unwrapped*.
2. Among mutual funds, fees vary significantly from fund to fund and by type of fund—even among comparable index funds. A study of 46,799 funds in 18 countries found some mutual fund total annual expense ratios to be significantly higher than 1 percent of assets: Australia, 1.60 percent; Canada, 2.68 percent; France, 1.13 percent; Germany, 1.22 percent; Switzerland, 1.42 percent; United Kingdom, 1.32 percent; United States, 1.4 percent. In addition to expense ratios, another charge, typically of 25 bps, is often levied as a 12b-1 fee by U.S. mutual funds. Ajay Khorana, Henri Servaes, and Peter Tufano, "Mutual Fund Fees Around the World," HBS Finance Working Paper 901023 (2007).
3. The impact of "only 1 percent" can accumulate over time into a very large number. In one example, two investors each start with $100,000 and add $14,000 each year for 25 years. One of the investors selects a manager who charges 1.10 percent, and the other investor pays only 0.10 percent—a difference of "only 1 percent." After 25 years, both have more than $1 million, but the difference between them is $255,423: over a quarter-million dollars separates $1,400,666 from $1,145,243.
4. Long ago, lawyers who created trusts for clients often provided trust administration too: collecting dividends and interest, redeeming bonds at maturity, filing tax returns,

and so forth. Because lawyers charged by the hour for such services, they also charged by the hour for investment management. In the first half of the last century, a few investment counsel firms were formed outside of law firms. Realizing that larger trusts should be charged more than smaller trusts as a matter of fairness, they shifted to charging fees based on *assets*. This would transform the industry from its low-profit past to one of the most profitable service businesses in the world, particularly after fees were raised as a percentage of assets from 0.10 percent to today's 0.50 to 1.25 percent.

5. Another exception may be found on wine lists at fine restaurants frequented by young hedge fund managers who may select wines by the price. Sardonic sommeliers have been known to reprice a few expensive wines, deliberately inflating prices to attract the attention of customers with a private need to prove to others that they can afford what they assume is the very best.

6. Major banks had credited part of the profits on commercial loans to their trust departments in recognition of the economic value of brokers' stable demand deposit. Banks saw this entrepreneurial profit—which they did not discuss with clients—as appropriate. When money market funds attracted these cash balances away from the banks, the impacted income was replaced by "NYSE equivalent" commissions added on to third-market trading with Weeden & Co. When negotiated rates later evaporated this source of income, J. P. Morgan decided to start charging fees for investment management.

7. The U.S. Labor Department's requiring more disclosure of fees to 401(k) sponsors and participants may help some to do so.

CHAPTER 22

PLANNING YOUR PLAY

YES, DEATH IS EVERY INDIVIDUAL'S ULTIMATE REALITY, BUT AS an *investor*, you may well be making too much of it. If, for example, you plan to leave most of your capital in bequests to your children or grandchildren, the appropriate time horizon for your family investment policy—even if you are well into your eighties or nineties—may be so long term that you'd be correct to ignore such investment conventions as "older people should invest in bonds for higher income and greater safety" or "to determine the percentage of your assets you should have in stocks, subtract your age from 100."

The wiser, better decision for you and your family might be to invest 100 percent in equities because your investing horizon may be far longer than your "living horizon." If the people you love (your family and heirs) or even the organizations you love (your favorite charities) are likely to outlive you—as they almost certainly will—perhaps you should extend your investment planning horizon to cover not just your own life span but theirs as well. For instance, if you are 40 years old and have a 5-year-old son, your real investment horizon may not be another 45 years (your own future life expectancy) but closer to the 80 more years your son is likely to live, particularly for any funds you plan to leave to him. Even if you are 75 years old, your investment horizon could be equally long if you have young grandchildren or a favorite charity.

We investors are mortal, but our investments don't know it and frankly don't care. (Remember another admonition from Adam Smith: "The stock doesn't know you own it.") This observation applies to all investments: stocks, bonds, buildings, and so forth. All have value today and will have a future value irrespective of who owns them. Therefore, investing should be done for investment reasons, not for such personal reasons as your age.

So don't change your investments just because you have reached a certain age or have retired. If you could afford fine paintings, you wouldn't change the ones you love the most simply because you'd reached retirement or celebrated your seventieth or eightieth birthday. It's the same with investments: Why not maintain a long-term strategy?

Compounding *is* powerful. Remember the grateful sultan who offered to reward his vizier generously for a good deed that had saved the sultan's empire. The vizier modestly offered to accept only one grain of wheat on the first square of a checkerboard, only two grains on the next, four grains on the third, eight grains on the fourth, and so on—and on and on. The crafty vizier said he had no need for a great reward and that the symbolism of this compounding giving would please his humble heart. Joyfully, the sultan seized upon this seemingly simple way to clear his obligation. But he did not reckon on the formidable power of compounding. Anything doubled 64 consecutive times will balloon—and balloon again. In the story, the few grains of wheat compounded to a total value that was greater than all the wealth in the empire. To defend his honor before Allah, the sultan ended up turning over the entire empire to the vizier.

All investors need to understand the impact on them and their investments from two kinds of risk: "market risk" and "inflation risk." Figure 22.1 shows how these two unavoidable risks trade off over 80 years. The first three columns show nominal returns with stocks producing nearly three *times* the returns of Treasury bills and T-bills never showing a loss. The second set of three columns—adjusted for inflation—tells a very different story. The real return on stocks is a full nine *times* the returns on T-bills.

Figure 22.1 Trade-off between market risk and inflation risk

	Nominal returns			Real returns		
1926–2006 total returns	Average annual return	Percent of years with negative return	Highest annual loss	Average annual return	Percent of years with negative return	Highest annual loss
T-bills	3.8%	0%	0.0%	0.8%	35%	−15.0%
Bonds	5.2	9	−2.3	2.1	38	−14.5
Stocks	10.5	30	−43.1	7.2	35	−37.3

Source: Adapted from Vanguard Investment Counseling & Research.

Note the percentage of years with negative returns. Before adjusting for inflation, T-bills never lose and stocks are negative 30 percent of the time, but *after* adjusting for inflation, T-bills and stocks *both* have negative returns 35 percent of the time. (Bonds are slightly worse.)

The message is not just how wonderfully compounding increases real wealth. The message has two parts, and the second is that inflation relentlessly destroys purchasing power almost as rapidly as economic gains build wealth. Only the real net gain is spendable.

Beware of the promotional materials and advertising that are deceiving investors with a Lorelei promise of phenomenal future riches without explaining the grimly negative impact inflation can have as the ruthless, unrelenting destroyer of capital: to purchase an item costing $100 in 1960 would cost more than $700 today.

Figure 22.2 The shrinking value of the dollar (1913–2011)

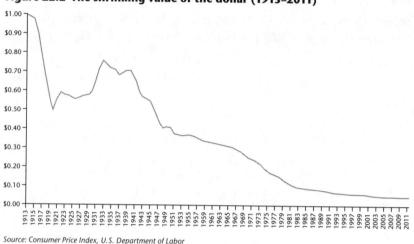

Source: Consumer Price Index, U.S. Department of Labor

The corrosive power of inflation can be the investor's real enemy. In just 20 years, as shown in Figure 22.2, the purchasing power of $1 shrank to 32 cents. The power of inflation to impose real harm on investments can be seen by studying the Dow Jones Industrial Average *after* adjustment for inflation. Note particularly:

- Over the five years from 1977 to 1982, the inflation-adjusted Dow took a five-year *loss* of 63 percent.
- Rational, long-term investors should know and remember that in the 15 years from the late 1960s to the early 1980s, the unweighted stock market, adjusted for inflation, plunged by about 80 percent. As a result, the decade of the 1970s was actually worse for investors than the decade of the 1930s.
- In 1993, the Dow was at last equal to its inflation-adjusted level at the peak of the highly speculative "bubble" market of 1929. Sixty-four years was a long, long time waiting to get even.

In developing a sound financial plan, investors will want to begin with good answers to these three overarching questions:

- Does my plan assure me of having enough income after inflation to pay for an appropriate standard of living during retirement? For most people, this "sufficiency of income" works out to 75 or 80 percent of preretirement spending plus 2 to 3 percent compounded annually to offset inflation.
- Will my financial reserves be sufficient to cover unexpected emergencies—usually healthcare—in old age? Beware! Eighty percent of a typical person's *lifetime* expenditures on health-care are spent in the last six months of life. Women live longer than men, and wives are often younger than their husbands, so most couples will want to pay particular attention to providing adequately for the wife's years as a widow.
- Will the remaining capital match our goals and intentions for giving to heirs and charities?

If these core questions are not answered fully and affirmatively, your plan needs to be reconsidered and changed, perhaps substantially. If change is called for, do it now so you'll have time on your side and working for you as long as possible. Write down your goals—with the target dates by which you intend to achieve them—so you can measure your actual progress compared with your explicit plan, because time is a key factor in all matters of investing. Investment decisions are not necessarily best when driven by noninvestment events such as the timing of a child's admission to college, the receipt of an inheritance, and the date of retirement, so separate *when* you invest from *how* you invest. Your investments do not know your wishes or intentions. The investment market won't adapt to you. So as an investor, you must adapt to the market.

Over your lifetime as an investor, your optimal investment program will change—and change again—partly because your circumstances and resources will change and partly because your objectives and priorities will change. But the more thoughtfully and soundly you plan and the further in advance you do your planning, the less you will need to change your plan as time passes. Planning a sound long-term investment program is often done best in 10-year chunks of time. This helps because working with decades reminds us that sound investing is inherently long term in nature. Of course, planning is only as useful as the actual implementation that follows. You will want to follow the wise coach's twin admonitions: "Plan your play *and* play your plan."

The first step is clear: get out of debt. It's a great, well-earned feeling when you achieve the first victory of paying off your school loans and the debts you incurred while you were setting up your first household. The key to getting out of debt is clear: *save!*

A lifetime based on the habit of thrift—spending less than you might and deferring the spending you do—is essential to saving. Those who assume or hope that their incomes will somehow outstrip their spending may believe in magic, but they are doomed to be disappointed, often grievously. "Pay yourself first" by putting money into savings on a regular basis. Dollar-cost averaging—a fixed dollar amount each month—is a good way to pay yourself first. And if your employer has a defined contribution retirement plan, be sure you make all the matchable contributions. Why leave free money on the table? Strive to participate at the maximum allowable level.

There's a big difference between deliberate, judicious borrowing and being in debt. The sensible borrower is comfortable because he or she has ample capacity to repay and, most important, decides or controls the timing of repayment. The debtor borrows only what a lender decides to lend and must repay at the time chosen by the lender. That's why borrowing with a mortgage is very different from "being in debt." (Just as borrowing differs from being in debt, retirement differs from old age. In retirement, you have more time for travel, reading, sports, and other interests. In old age, your body aches in different ways every day. And every night.)

Figure 22.3 tells an important story about inflation. The figures in the second row, labeled "nest-egg goal," are the amounts you would need to have saved by age 70 to have the inflation-adjusted equivalent of $35,000 in yearly spending money. (If you want $70,000 a year of spending money to sustain your lifestyle, multiply the figures in the second row by 2; if you want $105,000, multiply by 3, and so on.) Here's how to read the table:

- Find your present age in the top row.
- The nest-egg goal is the amount of capital you will need to accumulate to have an inflation-adjusted $35,000 to spend each year from age 65 on.
- The current savings on the left—ranging from zero to $250,000—is the annual amount invested tax-free at a return of 10 percent annually until you reach age 70. (Note: 10 percent is convenient for calculations, but almost certainly too high.)
- The rest of the table shows the amount you would need to save and invest to achieve your nest-egg goal.
- After retirement at age 70, the assumed returns average 7 percent. It is further assumed that by age 90 all your accumulated savings will have been spent. (Note: Many of us will live past 90.)

Figure 22.3 What it will take to get to there from here

Your current age	30	35	40	45	50	55	60
Nest-egg goal	$3 mil.	$2.5 mil.	$2.1 mil.	$1.7 mil.	$1.4 mil.	$1.1 mil.	$.94 mil.
Your current savings	How much you need to save annually						
$0	$6,890	$9,248	$12,524	$17,217	$24,300	$36,004	$58,995
$10,000	$5,868	$8,211	$11,463	$16,116	$23,125	$34,689	$57,367
$25,000	$4,334	$6,656	$9,872	$14,463	$21,363	$32,717	$54,926
$50,000	$1,777	$4,064	$7,220	$11,709	$18,427	$29,430	$50,857
$100,000	$0	$0	$1,916	$6,201	$12,554	$22,856	$42,720
$250,000	$0	$0	$0	$0	$0	$3,315	$18,308

Look at Figure 22.3 again. If your age is 35 (the second column), you'll need to accumulate $2.5 million by the time you reach age 70 to produce $35,000 a year of real spending money. The column shows—for each level of savings you've already accumulated—how much you'll have to save every year to achieve that goal.

Note the rather favorable assumptions: All your savings go into a tax-deferred account such as a 401(k) plan, where they are further assumed to compound at 10 percent annually—which certainly would be too high an expectation given the current economic outlook—until your retirement at age 70. Starting from present market levels, this may be possible, but it will certainly be challenging, even if you invest entirely in equities. In bonds, it simply cannot be done.

Remember algebra and solving equations with two unknowns? Did your course get to three unknowns? As investors, we are confronted by a much more complex challenge: to solve, or at least manage sensibly and rationally, a puzzle with five major unknowns, each of which is changing. The five unknowns are:

1. Rate of return on investments
2. Inflation
3. Spending
4. Taxes
5. Time

One analysis of a hypothetical 35-year investment plan started with the happy assumption that an investor began in 1964 with a cool $1 million.[1] The consequences of various investment programs were then examined. The nominal compound rates of return for this period were unusually favorable: 11.8 percent for stocks, 7.9 percent for bonds, and 6.8 percent for Treasury bills. The very pleasing—but, as we'll soon see, very deceptive—*theoretical* **final portfolio values** produced by the initial $1 million were:

Stocks	$55.0 million
Bonds	$15.5 million
T-bills	$10.7 million

Everyone's a winner! Or so it may appear. But here's how the results look *after* taxes:

Stocks	$30.2 million
Bonds	$6.6 million
T-bills	$4.4 million

What a difference those taxes make—particularly to bonds and T-bills. Note that the taxes assumed are minimal: the investor pays only federal taxes (no state or local taxes), has no other sources of taxable income, and files a joint return. For most investors who can invest $1 million, actual taxes are almost certain to be larger.[2]

Brace yourself for the impact of inflation because that's the way we convert nominal, or apparent, values into real money. The results are sobering. Here's the result *after* adjusting for inflation over the same 35 years:

Stocks	$5.4 million
Bonds	$1.2 million
T-bills	$0.8 million

Inflation, the data show, was a far larger problem for investors than taxes. In real purchasing power, bonds were only 20 percent ahead of the initial investment after a whole generation.[3] And T-bills were actually *behind* the starting line by 20 percent. That's why taxes and inflation are rightly known as fearsome "fiscal pirates."

It would be worse if the study had included realistic ownership costs such as mutual fund expenses and trading costs. Even the typical money market mutual fund charges roughly 0.5 percent per year in expenses, while bond funds charge up to 1 percent, and stock funds can charge as much as 1.5 percent. At those rates, you would have the following take-home results for your $1 million after deducting ownership costs:

Stocks	$1.8 million
Bonds	$755,000
T-bills	$589,000

Finally, as all investors were painfully reminded in 2008–2009, to earn the long-term "average" return, you would have needed enough fortitude to stay fully invested when the market plunged—tearing away at your portfolio *and* your determination to stay the course.

Spending is the next key factor. Again, time makes all the difference. Consider the consequences of two commonly used spending rules. One rule is to "limit spending in retirement to a moderate rate, such as 5 percent of your capital." If you followed this spending rule and your investments were entirely in bonds, your $1 million would have fallen in real purchasing power to just $200,000. The all-stock portfolio alternative is better, of course, but not by much. It would be up by about 30 percent, or less than 1 percent per year.

Another spending rule is to "limit spending to dividends and interest payments received." The investor following this rule starts out having significantly less to spend than does Mr. 5 Percent but, because dividends rise with corporate earnings, he soon catches up and goes ahead in spending more. Compounding is at work again.

Beware of a subtle danger. As an investor, you can almost always produce more income from your portfolio by investing more heavily in bonds or so-called income stocks with high dividend yields. But other investors are rational, and they'll let *you* get more today only if *they* can expect more tomorrow.[4] Thus, what appears to be high current income is partly a return of capital. For example, high-yield bonds may appear to pay 8 to 10 percent interest, but part of that payment is actually a return of the capital that's needed to offset the risk of occasional defaults. And every so often, one of those high-yield bonds does default.

What to do? In retirement, be conservative. Better safe than sorry. Ideally, limit annual withdrawals to 4 percent of a three-year moving average of your portfolio. This will protect your portfolio from inflation *and* from overspending. If you need to draw 5 percent each year, you'll want more portfolio stability. Put a rolling five years' expenditures in medium-term bonds and the rest in equities the year you retire. Each year, convert one more year's spending from equities to bonds *unless* the market is high and all the chatter is about good prospects, in which case you may be wise to convert to *two* years. Yes, this *is* a form of market timing, but it's seldom a bad idea to lean against the wind.

If you need to draw 6 percent of your retirement funds to live comfortably, you need to know you will be depleting your capital over time after adjusting for inflation—and eventually you *will* run out of money. If 6 percent won't meet your spending level, you owe it to yourself to cut back your spending to a level you can sustain. Nobody wants to outlive his or her resources.

Money links the past with the present and the present with the future as a medium of stored value. You can estimate the dollars you'll want to spend each year and, at a spending rate such as 4 percent, the total wealth required to produce the income to meet that level of spending. Determine what you have now and what you will save each year. Then see whether you can achieve your capital-accumulation objectives through a sensible investing program. If the first plan you design doesn't work, you need to go around again, planning to save more each year or work and save for more years *or* have less to live on. Be careful: being optimistic will not help. Be cautious and conservative with each assumption: your saving rate, your rate of return, and your spending.

For investors who depend on their annual income from investments, the good news is that while interest paid on T-bills will fluctuate from year to year and sometimes substantially, dividends on a portfolio of common stocks have almost never gone down and will generally rise at a little more than the rate of inflation.

By combining your saving and capital objectives with your realistic rate-of-return expectations and your available time horizon, you can work out your own investor's triangulation to see what amount of savings you will need to contribute each year to your long-term investment portfolio so you can achieve your realistic objectives for spendable money during retirement. (Your accountant or investment advisor can help you with the calculations.)

If you're surprised at how much you'll need to save and invest each year to meet your retirement spending goals, it may be modestly comforting to know that you are not alone. Retirement is expensive, partly because we are likely to live longer than our parents or grandparents (*and* incur more medical expenses in our later years because we have access to more expensive healthcare technology).

Investors may ponder the double-edged irony of death. If death comes sooner than expected and planned for, the resources saved over many years may go at least partially unused by the saver. If death comes much later than planned for, the saved-up resources may be too small, and a grim poverty can result. Be prudent, but don't be prudent to excess. You can save too much, and those who love you do not want you to suffer a life of self-enforced penury just so they can have extra money to spend after you're gone.

Your best bargain as a long-term investor is sound investment counseling that leads to the sensible long-term investing program most appropriate to your particular financial resources and responsibilities *and* to your particular risk tolerance, investment skills, and philanthropic aspirations. Ironically, most investors are unwilling to pay for real help in developing an optimal long-term investment program. This grievous "sin of omission" incurs great opportunity cost: the cost of missing out on what might easily have been.

Most investors could obtain very good investment counseling for a fee of less than $5,000 (paid only once each decade). Most investors will regularly pay more than $10,000 per million dollars every year in investment operating expenses such as brokerage commissions, advisory fees, and custody charges. It's ironic that investors will, however innocently, pay more for the lower value.

Suggestion: Pick one day a year (for example, your birthday, New Year's Day, or Thanksgiving) as your "day away for investing" and pledge to spend a few hours on that day every year quietly and systematically answering the following questions in writing. (After the first annual review, which may take several hours, you'll be updating the plan you wrote out in the prior year, so it won't take more than an hour. You can make that hour even more productive by rereading last year's plan a week or so before your "day away" so it will be in your subconscious, where so much good thinking and rethinking gets done.) These questions will help define and articulate your objectives:

- During retirement, how much income do I want to have each year in addition to Social Security and my employer's retirement benefit?[5]
- How many years will I be in retirement? (The key here is to estimate how long you'll live. Ask your doctor how to apply the average life span of your parents or grandparents to get a reasonable fix on your own "genetic envelope," appropriately adjusted for contemporary medicines and the healthfulness of your personal lifestyle.)
- What spending rule am I ready to live with and live by?

(Continued)

- How much capital will I need to provide amply for each year of my retirement?
- What savings and insurance will I need—inflation-adjusted—to cover full healthcare for my spouse and me?
- How much capital do I want to pass on to each member of my family and to special friends?
- How much capital do I hope to direct to my philanthropic priorities?

Next comes an easy-to-use solution to what most investors consider the truly difficult part of the problem: estimating long-term average annual rates of return on your investments. Here's one way.

First, recognize that over the long, long term—after adjusting for inflation—average returns for each type of investment have been approximately as follows:

Stocks	4.5 percent
Bonds	1.5 percent
T-bills	1.25 percent

Second, remember and act on the understanding that over the truly long term, the most important investment decisions seem almost obvious. Here are the two most important decision rules: Any funds that will stay invested for 10 years or longer should probably be in stocks. Any long-term investments in bonds are made as protection—not from the markets, but from your probable reaction to the markets when they are most upsetting. Any funds that will be invested for less than two to three years should be in money market instruments.

Next, prepare a complete inventory of your total investments, including stocks and bonds, equity in your home, and assets in any retirement plans.

Next, review your retirement income. (You can get help from your employer's human resources department or from your accountant.) Here are the obvious sources: pension benefits, Social Security, and income from your investments.

Last, review your desired bequests to family members (and others) and intended charitable contributions.

In investing over the longer run, benign neglect pays off. After basic decisions on long-term investment policy have been made with care and rigor, hold on to them. "Nervous money never wins," say poker players. And they should know. At the Kinderheim nursery in Vail, Colorado, the sign offers skiers a fine service at a great price: "Leave your kids for the day: $10." Then, mindful of the nursery's experience with overanxious parents, two alternatives are offered: "You watch: $10" and "You help: $25."

One final thought: before making any final commitments that are large in proportion to your total wealth, reread *King Lear.*

Notes

1. Alliance Bernstein, 1964–2000.
2. The effective tax rate on stocks is far lower than the effective tax rate on bonds because part of the return on stocks is market appreciation; the capital gains tax rate is lower and payment is often deferred for many years, until you decide to sell. A reasonable estimate of the actual or effective federal tax rate on returns from stocks is under 15 percent, about half the tax rate on income from bonds or bills.
3. Note that in all but one year since 1950, if you invested in tax-free municipal bonds and then held and reinvested for

20 years, you *lost* money. In that one favorable initial investment year, you made 0.01 percent annually after inflation, but that was before management or custody expenses.

4. The market is a place where other participants will let you have more of what you want as an investor if, and only if, you let them get more of what they want.

5. Be sure everyone you know understands that Social Security benefits change wonderfully if you do not claim as early as possible at the age of 62, but wait as long as possible to age 70 1/2. Waiting 7 1/2 years increases your annual benefits by 76% (inflation protected) all your life.

CHAPTER 23

DISASTER AGAIN AND AGAIN

O N DECEMBER 11, 2008, 8,000 INVESTORS—FORMERLY HAPPY TO BE receiving reports of their year-in-year-out returns of 10 percent or better on a secretive "inside the market" operation they had been privately let in on by well-connected friends—found they had actually been victims of a giant Ponzi scheme run by Bernard L. Madoff. *Fifty billion dollars* was Madoff's initial estimate of how much money he had vaporized. For Madoff's victims, it was a personal disaster.

Madoff told clients he specialized in "split-strike conversion" strategies using derivatives to minimize risk—strategies he made clear were so proprietary that he would not discuss them in any detail for fear others would copy his technique and ruin everything for everyone. He claimed to buy stocks and sell put and call options on them. (Selling the calls meant not participating in a price increase beyond a set amount, while the puts protected against a price decrease by a set amount.) To protect his secret process, Madoff, who had been chairman of Nasdaq and a frequent expert advisor to the Securities and Exchange Commission and had served on several philanthropic boards, kept a tight inner circle: audits were conducted by a tiny three-person accounting firm, and all trading was executed through his own captive dealership.

Like Charles Ponzi in the 1920s, Madoff had been paying out money to withdrawing investors not from accumulating profits but from new cash coming in from new investors. Those content to receive 10 percent or so *every* year—at which rate money doubles in just over seven years, doubles again in the next seven, *and* then doubles again—got comforting monthly reports on how steadily their fortunes were compounding. Most preferred to leave their money with Madoff, presumably steadily multiplying. Consistency was remarkable: only 11 monthly losses from 1992 to 2008.

The lesson for all: if it seems too good to be true and "this time it's different," it *is* too good to be true. So don't bite. Sure, Bernie was charming, modest, and bright. Sure, it was a family firm. Sure, you got introduced through a friend of a friend. Sure, you felt certain you could trust him. Everybody seemed to. Ten percent was very good—good enough to attract investors, but not beyond plausibility. The SEC had been "tipped" several times but had not found any wrongdoing. Bernie had friends in a variety of charities and in other high places.

* * * * *

On October 6, 2008, Iceland—geographically remote near the Arctic Circle and historically detached from the rest of the world, with a hardy population of just 320,000—suddenly became the epicenter of financial violence. Icelanders, traditionally savers and famously stubborn while enduring serial hardships, had had a national pension system sufficient to ensure security for all their elderly. All that suddenly changed when Prime Minister Geir Haarde went on TV to make two astonishing announcements: the nation was virtually bankrupt, and the government was taking over all three banks.

In the years before Haarde's painful broadcast, Iceland's bold, self-congratulating young businessmen, who called themselves "Viking Raiders," had borrowed heavily to acquire. But suddenly, all lending had stopped cold, and currency exchange was not possible. The nation was bankrupt and the three banks were bankrupt, as were many Icelandic families and businesses. Iceland's krona was frozen in the world's capital markets. Easy access to loans and 100 percent mortgages—payable in foreign currencies *and* ominously indexed to inflation that had shot up locally to 20 percent annually—had allowed young people to buy homes, cars, and furniture with debt. Retirement funds that had been sufficient to ensure security for all Icelanders were suddenly cut in half—and then cut even more.

In the seven years after the national banks had been privatized, Iceland's financial institutions had borrowed $75 billion abroad—many times the national gross domestic product (GDP) and $250,000 for every person in Iceland. (By comparison, America's horrendous $700 billion financial rescue package was "only" 5 percent of GDP.) Some blamed the Viking Raiders; some blamed lax regulators. Never before had any nation, or any country's population, been trapped so cataclysmically in the stark realities of being deeply mired in debt to strangers.

That's why the head of government went on television to address the nation: "Fellow countrymen . . . if there was ever a time when the Icelandic nation needed to stand together and show fortitude in the face of adversity, then this is the moment. I urge you all to guard that which is most important in the life of every one of us, to protect those values which will survive the storm now beginning. I urge families to talk together and not allow anxiety to get the upper hand, even though the outlook is grim for many. We need to explain to our children that the world is not on the edge of a precipice, and we all need to find an inner courage to look to the future. . . . Thus, with Icelandic optimism, fortitude, and solidarity as weapons, we will ride out the storm. God bless Iceland." All across Iceland, silence followed as the grim reality sank in.

There was no sympathy for Iceland or its banks when 500,000 British and Continental savers—individuals, charities, and local authorities—realized that they had just lost $15 billion, or an average of $30,000 per loser. Restoring those losses would take longer than most investors' lifetimes.

* * * * *

The Madoff and Iceland experiences are both different in one profound way from the horrendous global market meltdown of 2008. The Madoff and Iceland losses were permanent; that money was gone forever. Markets, on the other hand, do recover, so the great risk to individual investors, as it has been so often before and will be again and again, is not that the market can and will plummet but that investors will get frightened into liquidating their investments at or near the bottom and will miss all the recovery, thus turning the temporary market loss into a permanent capital loss. This happens to all too many investors in every terrible market.

Market prices, as we all know, are driven by buying and selling. The only way to push prices up to peak levels is for the largest possible number of investors with the most money—including borrowed money—to reach their highest conviction that stocks are an imperative "buy." And the only way to drive prices down to their lowest level is to have the largest possible aggregate amount of insistent, concentrated selling. That's what happened all over the world in the fall of 2008.

It had all started with a high level of confidence in the outlook for the economy and corporate profits and a confident view that risks were low. In stock market after stock market around the world, prices were between "fully priced" and "high." There were few bargains. Those prices might have been okay if the underlying economies and corporate earnings had continued to advance. But in one of the sharpest-ever reversals of expectations, investors, banks, individuals, and governments, which had been financing expansion with debt, slammed into reverse.

Trust disappeared, taking credit with it. The culprit at the center was the ever-increasing use of leverage, particularly in the

United States. Easy credit terms, high property appraisals, low interest rates, derivatives, the rising mass of leveraged hedge funds, and the SEC's authorizing Wall Street dealers to increase their use of debt were major ingredients in the cheap-credit cocktail. Republicans, determined to deregulate the economy, joined forces with Democrats interested in helping more families get mortgages, and agreed to change the home loan regulations and increase credit from Fannie Mae and Freddie Mac. This led eventually to "ninja" loans to borrowers with no income, no jobs, and no assets, who assumed they could speculate profitably on rising house prices. Packages of inappropriate mortgage loans were securitized and sold all over the world with credit ratings that were far too favorable, based on excessively high property valuations or appraisals and credit default insurance, which proved to be disastrously underwritten. When the mortgage securities' values plunged, the pain spread everywhere.

Economic, market, and psychological dominoes pushed one another over. Credit ratings were found faulty, and security values were cut. Confidence disappeared. Credit markets froze. Leverage was pulled away from hedge funds, and dealers were forced to sell. Investor withdrawals from these funds compounded the selling pressure. Massive, urgent selling swept the markets as hedge funds and others dumped stocks to raise cash to meet lenders' insistent demands and anticipations of a further drop in share prices. Credit markets stayed frozen. Prominent financial institutions failed. Government rescues collided with politics. Forced selling and anticipation of more hard selling to come dominated markets that were already dropping because of fears of recession. In 14 months, the U.S. stock market lost *half* its value—more than $7 trillion.[1]

Credit rating agencies were severely criticized for failing to understand the true creditworthiness of the packaged subprime loans that they had been rating triple-A. Great corporations like GE could not even refinance short-term commercial paper, and

Lehman Brothers failed. Wachovia and Washington Mutual went into shotgun mergers. AIG, the nation's largest insurance company, was taken over by the government. Comparable difficulties beset commercial banks, central banks, and governments in one nation after another.

The "Now what?" question every investor was asking during the crisis would bring a new clarity to the true meaning of risk. In its classic and most powerful definition, risk is a function of unacceptable *permanent* loss. Madoff and Iceland exemplified that kind of risk. So too did the destruction of Lehman Brothers and others. And so did individual investors who sold off their stocks in a "flight to safety," making their personal market disasters permanent. For long-term investors, as always, the worst mistake was getting out of stocks: locking the barn door *after* the animals had run off. In the jargon of Wall Street, this was a *big* "black swan" event—black swans being creatures that, though rare, do occur once in a while.

Note

1. Yet the pain, awful as it was, was not as great—inflation-adjusted—as it had been in the unrelenting stock market collapse of the 1970s.

CHAPTER 24

GETTING RIGHT ON 401(K) PLANS

MILLIONS OF EMPLOYEES OF COMPANIES THAT HAVE SWITCHED from traditional pension plans to 401(k) plans are going to have serious financial trouble in retirement unless senior managements at many companies decide to make changes soon by adopting the "guided 401(k)."

The 401(k) problem is simple, stark, and steadily getting worse. Fortunately, senior management can solve most of the problem with 401(k)s by making two kinds of changes that major companies have already made:

- Make all best practices standard
- Reset expectations for the age of retirement

As more observers are recognizing with increasing alarm, a major problem—widespread retirement *in*security—is coming our nation's way unless we take corrective action soon. While most people in the economic top one-third of affluence will be okay, the problem seriously threatens the lower two-thirds—and particularly the bottom third. They risk experiencing a seriously negative trifecta: being old, poor, and alone. This could take us back to the early 1950s in social injustice, a problem we worked hard to put far behind us. It does not need to happen. We can prevent this painful problem *if* we act sensibly and soon.

Can you answer these key questions about retirement security quickly and confidently?

- When was 65 set as the right age for retirement?
- If the ratio of working years to retirement years were the same today as it was back when Social Security was enacted in 1935, what would today's full retirement age be?
- What is the difference in your Social Security benefits if you claim them at age 70 versus 62?
- How many of us will require "assisted living"?
- How many American workers know how to save and plan and invest for their retirement reasonably well?

Here are the answers:

- Age 65 was set in Germany by chancellor Otto von Bismarck back in the 1880s—over 130 years ago—when life expectancy was below age 50. It is now 86 and rising.
- If we kept the same ratio of working years to retirement years as in 1935, today's retirement age would be a little over 70.
- It's 76 percent! Waiting to claim Social Security benefits at 70 instead of 62 increases those annual benefits by 76 percent— and they are inflation-protected *and* continuing for life.
- About half the couples in their 60s will see at least one of them requiring costly assisted-living care for at least six months.
- Way too few. With the shift from traditional defined-benefit to defined-contribution, or 401(k), plans, millions of workers— without the necessary investment experience and with all too many predatory salespeople looking for them—must decide by themselves how much to save and how to invest to cover their costs in retirement. The history of individual investor decisions is *not* comforting.

The main 401(k) problem is not with plan design or the intentions of plan sponsors. The problem is with *implementation*. In most cases, all the important decisions are made not by the company but by each employee. But most of us are not trained, prepared for, or skilled at making the key decisions. So as the evidence now shows, we make all-too-human mistakes—and we make them at every stage.

Individual 401(k) participants make mistakes at as many as eight different stages: (1) not participating in their company's plan; (2) not "matching the match"; (3) not increasing contributions (ideally to 12 percent or more of compensation) as their pay increases; (4) borrowing or taking money out of their 401(k)s to cover expenses between jobs; (5) changing investments—buying high and selling low—as markets gyrate; (6) retiring too soon "because we can"; (7) withdrawing too much each year in retirement; and (8) not anticipating those ballooning late-in-life costs for healthcare and assisted living.

The result: If we leave things as they are, millions of workers will have far too little for a comfortable retirement. They will be "living too long" and running out of savings. Contrary to the American Dream, many will find themselves on their own, too old to return to work, with too little money *and* with late-in-life costs for healthcare and assisted living looming ahead. Our seniors will be demanding, "*You* could see the problem coming— why didn't you tell *me*?"

Using lessons from behavioral economics, leading companies have found and adopted an effective set of best practices. Instead of leaving employees on their own to analyze complex questions and make each important decision, including whether to *opt in*, these companies guide their employees to best practices. Each employee either accepts the best practice or decides to *opt out* and make his or her own decisions. Experience shows that this simple switch from "opt in" to "opt out" greatly increases the number of employees who participate *and* save enough *and* invest sensibly. If we made the proven best practices standard, many millions more American workers would be on their way to enjoying retirement security.

Table 24.1, based on the experiences of companies that have made the change, shows the splendid impact on participation by simply shifting the worker's decision from "opt in" to "opt out."

Table 24.1 How participation changes with opt out vs. opt in

	Opt-in participation	Opt-out participation	Changes in participation
Join plan	75%	95%	+20
Match the match	70%	95%	+25
Escalate contributions	30%	80%	+50
Sensible investing	30%	90%	+60

The second major problem is that many workers assume 65 (or even younger) is the "right" age for retirement. A brief look at history—and a look into the future—will show why this assumption is way out of date *and* dangerous.

Age 65 started being used for retirement in Bismarck's Germany in the 1880s, when average life expectancy at birth was only 45 (and at 65 only 18 months). Given the historical precedent in Germany and the United Kingdom, retirement at 65 was included when the United States established Social Security in 1935—when life expectancy at 65 was six years. Today life expectancy at 65 is 20 years for men and 22 years for women (25 percent of couples will see one or more members live into their nineties).

The shift from defined-benefit plans—arguably the best consumer financial service ever developed—to 401(k) plans cannot be stopped. Today far fewer people work for just one company for their full career, so they want portability. And plan sponsors are understandably concerned about costs. But while accepting reality is important, that does not mean accepting all the current imperfections in 401(k) plans when we know how to make them work so much better.

Most companies want to do the right thing in their retirement programs because they care about their workers' welfare and know that a strong retirement plan attracts good workers and fosters good morale. When setting policies for 401(k) plans and balancing the interests of employees, retirees, and owners, each company has its own priorities. This has resulted in a great variety of practices by different companies for good reasons. Still, experience with 401(k)s reveals a series of opportunities for many companies to improve their plans by adopting the best practices of leading corporations.

Let's begin with an emphatic declaration: none of the following recommendations, all based on proven best practices of leading corporations sponsoring 401(k) plans, need be mandatory for individual *participants*. But they *should* be required in each plan and be *voluntary* for individual participants, with an "opt out" provision to protect each individual's freedom of choice.

Twenty years of retirement are expensive—far too expensive for many individuals to pay for with declining benefits from Social Security and inadequate funds in their 401(k)s. The median 401(k) balance for a 65-year-old American is currently only $120,000. With a 4 percent drawdown—and market returns reduced by 2 percent to offset inflation—that provides only $4,800 a year. Adding Social Security and 401(k) draws, the average combined payout would be a serious drop from median earned income for active workers of about $63,000 at 65.

The benefits of working to age 70 are substantial. Start with Social Security. Close examination of Social Security benefits reveals an important reality. Due to past changes, the financially optimal age for retirement has already shifted from 65 to 70. While the Social Security Administration still calls 65 "full retirement age" and workers can, if they want, claim benefits even earlier, at 62, the financial rewards of working until 70 are eye-popping. Social Security benefits begun at 70 are a stunning 76 percent *higher* than benefits claimed at 62. (As always, these benefits are inflation-protected *and* continue as long as you live.)

In addition to the 76 percent increase in Social Security benefits, working to age 70 gives employees eight years during which they can make new contributions to a 401(k) *and* saves them eight years of payouts *not* taken. Together, these two changes can *double* the size of an employee's 401(k) balance before including any investment return. Adding in investment returns, that 401(k) balance can more than double and, depending on investment returns, possibly triple over those eight years, to an average of about $360,000. This would provide the average retiree with an additional $12,000 to $15,000 every year.

The combination of 76 percent higher Social Security benefits *and* a tripling of 401(k) payouts would assure many retirees of a financially comfortable retirement. Given awareness of these financial realities, who would *not* want to add one-fifth to their working and saving years to enjoy up to three *times* as much annual income in every year of retirement?

Though estimates differ on how many millions of American workers will have inadequate savings for financially secure retirements—because they differ on whether "income replacement" of 60 percent, 70 percent, or 80 percent of preretirement income is enough for comfort—all experts agree that unless we make changes soon, millions of American workers will have too little for the comfortable retirements they are now expecting. The realities of practice are falling way short of the theory and early promises of the 401(k) plan that increasingly dominates corporate retirement programs.

Saving is particularly hard for those who fall *below* the median income, which is now just over $50,000. Deciding how much to save is challenging for almost everyone. And investing wisely for the long-term, distant future is very hard for all of us. Yet today many 401(k) plans, as presently implemented, leave all the saving and investing decisions up to each individual plan participant. Given what we know about the mistakes many individuals make with their investments, we should anticipate trouble—and the trouble is snowballing and bearing down on us.

America can change the course of retirement history by being sure that each worker understands the major benefits of working longer *and* that employers with 401(k) plans—to get the tax advantages on which our nation now spends over $160 billion a year—commit to using the proven best practices of automatic enrollment; automatic "match the match"; automatic increases in savings, such as one-quarter of each pay raise going into savings; and investing in "target date" or age-appropriate balanced investment using low-cost index funds. The net result of making these changes would shift millions of retirees from having too little to having enough for a decent, financially secure retirement.

To see why everyone who can participate in such plans should do so, and to the maximum extent allowed, just look at Figure 24.1. Note the huge impact of starting early and compounding!

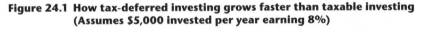

Figure 24.1 How tax-deferred investing grows faster than taxable investing (Assumes $5,000 invested per year earning 8%)

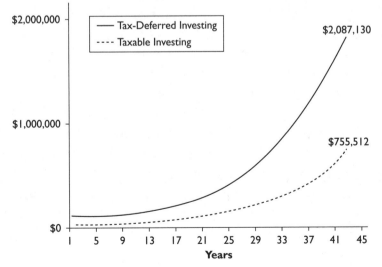

Here is a series of recommendations. Please give each one your serious consideration:

1. Do not confuse loyalty to your company with investment wisdom. Many 401(k) investors invest in their employer's stock because they know and trust the company. Don't do it. You already have a major economic dependency on that one company through your job, so adding more to that economic relationship is *not* smart diversification.

2. Do not change investment managers. The best way *not* to change managers is to index.

3. Do not "play the market." Making more than one change per decade is almost certainly too much and can be costly.

4. Sign up for automatic deductions from your income—before you see the money, so saving is almost easy—and arrange to increase your rate of saving each time you get a pay raise.

5. Get your children or grandchildren started early. Once they begin earning income on their own, you can make an IRA contribution of as much as $5,000 per year to each child or grandchild, up to the amount of their earned income. One great concern is that many young 401(k) investors keep surprisingly large proportions of their initial portfolios in money market or "stable value" funds, even though they may be decades away from retirement. They *are* saving, but they are *not* investing—as they really must to assure themselves of adequate retirement security.

6. If your employer offers a "life cycle" or "target date" fund with the mix of stock and bond index funds managed in proportions that change sensibly as you move toward retirement, give this hassle-free option serious consideration.

7. Be sure you invest enough each year to take full advantage of your employer's matching contribution. (Most companies have, and want their workers to use, a matching

contribution, so you can double your own money immediately. That's a great way to start.)

8. Fees matter a lot—and fees can differ a lot. Black Rock, Northern Trust, State Street, and Vanguard charge less than 0.1 percent for their index funds. Another index manager charges—10 *times* as much—a 50 percent higher 0.15 percent *plus* a 0.35 percent 12b-1 marketing fee *plus* other expenses that can total over 1 percent. And other providers—usually insurance companies serving small plans—charge even more! Over time, those differences in fees can compound into large differences as shown in Figure 24.2.

Figure 24.2 How high fees can erode performance

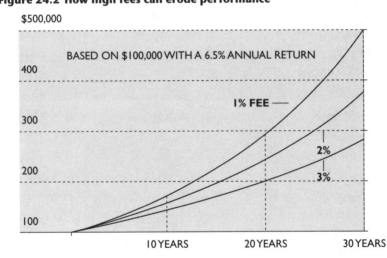

9. Roth IRAs make sense for young people. Most mutual fund companies provide plain-language guides for deciding whether a Roth is right for you.

10. Some worry philosophically about "paternalism." Some worry about possible future class action suits because of

regulatory uncertainty. And some worry about too much government regulation. All these concerns would evaporate if Congress provided a "safe harbor" for any company that adopts the already established norms of best practices.

ENDGAME

INVESTORS CAN—AND CERTAINLY SHOULD—SUBSTANTIALLY increase their lifetime financial and emotional success by paying appropriate attention to what all chess players know is important: the endgame.

If you are fortunate, as many Americans are, to have earned or inherited more than you need to live out your own definition of the good life, you'll have the opportunity *and* the responsibility to decide where and how to direct the funds not spent. Most affluent people focus on two quite different kinds of beneficiaries, which both can be deeply meaningful: people (usually family members) and values (usually such philanthropic organizations as colleges, schools, hospitals, and religious organizations).

Deciding what will be done with your capital to maximize its real value can be just as important as deciding how to save, accumulate, and invest. Providing for your retirement is one of three important challenges and opportunities. Bequests and gifts to those you love are another. The third, "giving back" to our society, can be exciting and fulfilling.

Because money is such an effective way to store or transfer value, an investor with a surplus beyond his or her own lifetime's wants and needs will have the opportunity to make a difference to others. Blessed is the investor whose assets do good; cursed are those who, despite their best intentions, cause harm.

Wealth *is* power—both the power to do good and the power to do harm. Greater wealth means greater power. Investors who have enjoyed substantial financial success should give careful consideration, no matter what their hopes or intentions, to whether the amount of wealth they can transfer to their children might do real harm by distorting their offspring's values and priorities or by taking away their descendants' joy in making their own way in life. While Mae West was speaking for herself when she announced that "too much of a good thing can be *wunnerful*," a giant inheritance is usually *not* wonderful for your children. All too often, "poor little rich kids" are miserable.

"Successful families make thoughtful choices concerning their wealth and think about the effect of their decisions on the lives of their children and their spouses and their grandchildren," says Harvard's philanthropic advisor, Charles W. Collier. "Most importantly, they talk openly with their children, at age-appropriate times, about all the issues surrounding the family's true wealth and give their younger family members as much responsibility as they can manage as soon as possible."

As Collier explains in his guidebook *Wealth in Families*, "According to Aristotle and his latter-day student, Thomas Jefferson, the 'pursuit of happiness' has to do with an internal journey of learning to know ourselves and an external journey of service of others."

Before outlining some of the possibilities for transfers within the circle of those you love or feel responsibility for, let's remember that money has powerful symbolic meaning. Psychiatrists marvel that although patients talk rather extensively and relatively early in therapy about relationships with parents, childhood experiences, central hopes and fears, and even very private matters such as dreams and sexual experiences, the one subject almost never discussed is money. Money is often the thermonuclear device among symbols, and it symbolizes a lot, in different—and often quite unexpected—ways for different people.

Most people find it very difficult to discuss money matters openly, fully, rationally, and wisely. Therefore, it's best to be especially thoughtful and cautious when making plans about how your money will pass on to others. Yes, it's your money now and while you live, but neither of these cheerful current realities will last forever.

You'll want to get expert legal advice when formulating a sound estate plan, but here are some items for consideration, recognizing that each person will have his or her own objectives and resources and will want to make his or her own decisions:

1. You can give up to $14,000—without tax—to *each* person you wish *every* year. Married couples can give $28,000 annually to each person. For most investors, over time, these annual gifts can be the central, even dominant part of a lifelong estate planning and family investment management program. (Gifts to young children can be made in care of a parent as custodian under the Uniform Transfers to Minors Act.) A main advantage of these gifts is completely sidestepping the estate tax when you die.

   You might concentrate on your children. Such gifts can really mount up, partly because the future investment income earned on the sums given is taxed at the child's tax rate, which is almost certain to be far lower than yours. Over 20 years, $14,000 given annually can, with sensible investing, accumulate to the better part of $500,000; $28,000 a year from both parents could produce $1 million or more. Again, the keys to success are *time* and *compounding*, so plan well, start early, and stay with your plan.

2. You have a lifetime total limit of $1 million on other tax-free gifts to individuals. If you have sufficient capital, a serious look at estate tax tables—particularly at the highest incremental rate you're likely to incur—will strongly encourage you to use this right to give. And contemplation of the

cumulative consequences of compound interest will encourage you to exercise this right relatively early in life.

3. Despite Elizabethan laws against "perpetuities," the Internal Revenue Service allows you to put up to $1 million into a generation-skipping tax-free family fund. (Your children can decide how this trust's assets will be divided among their descendants.) Gift or estate taxes must be paid *before* the assets pass to this fund. However, once these initial taxes are paid, the assets can grow and accumulate tax free for several generations within your family, typically for 80 to 100 years. Remember that *if* investments increase by 7 percent per annum after income tax, they will double every 10 years, so $1 million can become $1 billion in 100 years (before adjusting for inflation, of course). In the meantime, this family fund can operate as a "family bank" by making distributions or loans to family members as needed.

4. A curious provision called a "qualified personal residence trust" enables you to transfer ownership of your house to your children and live in your home rent free for a set period of time (such as 15 years). You save substantially on estate taxes—unless you die before the trust matures—while ownership passes to your children.

   A home can be transferred as a taxable gift valued at only 20 to 30 percent of the current market value. The IRS considers the taxable present value of the gift to be just the value of the children's right to take possession at the end of, say, the 15-year term of the trust. (The discount to a low present value is the obverse of the powerful accumulation or growth generated by compound interest.)

5. If you wish to transfer substantial sums to your descendants but you worry about distorting their values and lives with too much money at too early an age—before they reach "fiscal maturity"—consider an arrangement used by Jackie

Onassis (but reversed by her children under an optional provision in her will that you can leave out of yours).

Here's the general idea: a trust can be established for 20 to
30 years with interim annual distributions of income payable to your favorite school or charity (either at a set dollar
amount or as a percentage of the trust's assets), with the
trust corpus (the body of the money, from the Latin word for
"body") paid, after the 20- to 30-year term you selected, to
your chosen beneficiaries, such as your children.

There's no estate tax, and a gift tax is paid only on the
estimated net present value of the trust's corpus after dis-
counting at the IRS's prescribed interest rate—an amount
that is only a fraction of the probable market value of the
corpus 20 to 30 years from now.

If you are concerned about the harm that might be done
by a *current* wealth transfer to a 30- to 35-year-old benefi-
ciary, but are sanguine that the same transfer in the *future*
would not harm the values of that same person at age 60 or
65, this sort of trust can be an effective way to transfer substantial wealth with minimal tax. Noting that the key figures
are all based on estimates of market valuations far in the
future, the wise investor will want to work out the specific
term of the trust and the investment policy under several
different scenarios and select the choice with which he or
she feels most comfortable.

6. It takes more capital to deliver $1 million after taxes as a
   bequest ($2.2 million) than as a gift ($1.55 million). Gift taxes
   are assessed on the gift without regard to other taxes paid,
   while estate taxes are based on the whole estate before taxes
   are deducted.

7. Curiously, and quite accurately, estate lawyers will advise
   that one of the best assets to use for charitable giving at your
   death may be your currently tax-exempt defined contribution

retirement fund: your 401(k), 403(b), IRA, or profit-sharing plan. This surprising anomaly is true because these assets must be included in your estate—subject not only to the estate tax but also to income taxes as distributions are paid out to beneficiaries as of your date of death. Both of these taxes can be avoided if you decide to donate the capital to charity.

Inverted, or upside-down, reasoning can be a usefully mind-freeing way to explore any complex issue. Investors can think of estate taxes not as a tax on *wealth* but as a tax on *caution*—your reluctance to make irrevocable decisions while living (particularly long, long before your death) about the distribution of your wealth. If you are willing and able to make irrevocable decisions now regarding the long-term future disposition of your capital, you can save substantially on taxes. And, as always, a penny saved is a penny earned.

Most investors are *not* willing to make these wealth-distribution decisions—yet. But please remember: only if you are willing to make decisions about the future now can the power of compound interest be used for the maximum period to have the maximum impact on achieving your carefully considered goals and objectives.[1] Maximizing your lifetime financial success has five stages:

- Earning
- Saving
- Investing
- Contributing
- Estate planning

Ideally, you will maximize achievement in each area—according to your own values—within the feasible set of opportunities available to you as you enjoy a full and balanced life. As with other areas of investing, it's wise to plan ahead, to be conservative (within limits), and to make productive use of time by beginning early and sustaining your commitments over as long a period as you can.

Education is usually your best investment, whether you invest in your own or in that of your children or grandchildren—or in educating a great kid whose family can't afford the education of his or her choice. Education increases earning power over many years *and* leads to richer, more enjoyably interesting lives with more freedom of choice. The other "best investment" is staying in good health through exercise, weight control, not smoking, and the like. You really can live longer and better—and at a lower total cost.

Investors who have conscientiously worked to *maximize* the amount of their savings and investments will also want to pay comparable attention to *minimizing* the diversion of funds caused by taxes, particularly estate taxes. This effort will help achieve *your* fiscal objectives in support of *your* main values.

In thinking about bequests to children and grandchildren, wise people focus on deciding what amount would be the best—as distinct from the most. Consider, please, the following poetic doorway to wisdom from Kurt Vonnegut:

> True story, word of honor. Joseph Heller, an important and funny writer, now dead, and I were at a party given by a billionaire on Shelter Island.
>
> I said, "Joe, how does it make you feel to know that our host only yesterday may have made more money than your novel *Catch-22* has earned in its entire history?" And Joe said, "I've got something he can never have." And I said, "What on earth could that be, Joe?" And Joe said, "The knowledge that I've got enough."
>
> Not bad! Rest in peace!

Two of the wealthiest people in the United States have decided to leave only moderate amounts to their children. Warren Buffett says that the perfect amount to leave children is "enough money so they would feel they could do anything, but not so much that they could do nothing." Buffett's friend Bill Gates echoes that view. "Part of the reason for believing that my wealth should be given back to society," says Gates, "and not in any substantial percentage be passed on to my children, is that I don't think it would be good for them. They really need to get out and work and contribute to society. I think that's an important element of a fulfilling life."[2]

When thinking about gifts and bequests to children, parents know that each child is a unique individual and may be quite different from his or her siblings in wealth, earnings, or financial needs. This can make it tough to decide between "fair" and "equal." The best financial plans resolve the natural tension or dynamic between each person being an individual and each being part of a family. Capital transfers can divide or enhance family relationships. What's right for taxes may or may not be right for the individuals in your family.

Most families have core values—such as the importance of philanthropy or entrepreneurship—that need money for realization. Sharing and developing those values can be a vital part of the next generation's growing-up years. The meaning you give to wealth says a lot about who you are and the way you'll be seen and remembered. That's why developing shared values with your family and articulating guiding principles that will inform your family's choices can be so important. Suggestion: take time to introduce your will with a page or more sharing your values and feelings with those you love. It may be your last opportunity to be heard.[3] If you have surplus funds beyond the amount you wish to transfer to members of your family and others you care for, don't overlook the profoundly rewarding opportunities you may have created for yourself to cause good things to happen through philanthropy.

"Giving money away to charity" puts the whole proposition the wrong way. Instead, think in terms of imaginatively and vigorously *investing* your money—the stored values you and your skills have created over many years—to make good things happen for and through the people and organizations you care about. You can derive a great deal of pleasure and personal fulfillment in the process of making a positive difference in other people's lives.

People inclined to think they made their fortunes by themselves are *partly* right. Most fortune builders *did* work hard, take risks, and overcome major barriers. Still, they might well ponder how well they would have done if they had been born in central Africa or western China or a variety of other places. Most Americans know that we owe a large fraction of our success to our dynamic economy and its myriad market opportunities, our educational system, and the ability to let investment values compound without tax until they are sold—and then to pay only capital gains taxes.

No man or woman is an island; as John Donne understood, we *are* all part of the main. Those with modest wealth may focus on their families and a few local charities, while those with more wealth may respond to all of humanity and their ability to invest wealth creatively in reducing painful problems or increasing opportunities. On Abraham Maslow's famous needs hierarchy, after and above "self-actualization" are *transcendences.* These needs can be realized when we move beyond ourselves to see a greater fulfillment linked directly to serving the needs and hopes of others.

Givers have learned how greatly they can enjoy seeing the wealth they have created—the stored-up consequences of their hard work, imagination, and good fortune—come to life *again* by reducing constraints on individuals or society and enabling good things to happen during their lives in ways that matter to them. As the old saying has it, "You can't take it with you." Those who give something back invariably speak of this dimension of their lives with genuine satisfaction. And those who contribute even more find they enjoy even greater satisfaction.

Select the actions or changes that would give you deep spiritual satisfaction or pleasure to see coming to fruition, and make these good things come true by committing your capital to help make them happen. Like many others, you may find you enjoy great gratification in converting your financial resources into actions and values you truly care about. Here are some opportunities to make an impact:

- Establish scholarships for young people with great talent who aspire to make significant contributions in the arts, science, business, or government.
- Contribute to scholarships for young people who've gotten a bad deal in life and need someone's help to get on the right road. (If you don't have a particular school in mind, consider Kentucky's Berea College, which accepts *only* kids who can't afford a college education.)
- Provide financial support for advancing science, medicine, or social justice.
- Support hospitals, shelters, and other institutions to help those in severe need or those who served in our military.
- Supply funding for the arts—music, dance, theater, painting, sculpture—that enrich our lives.
- Help make your community a better place to live in by being one of the "go-to" leaders who commit time and money to make good things happen.

Your greatest satisfaction may come from serving a major national institution, a global organization, or a small entity in your neighborhood. Experienced charitable activists agree that while contributing money is important, even greater enjoyment and satisfaction result when they also make a substantial commitment of their time, skills, and energy. Don't leave this important part of your life experience "in storage" for someone else to enjoy doing after you're gone.

Contributing your time, talent, and money can be profoundly gratifying in two ways. For you, there is great personal satisfaction in seeing how real, living people and organizations benefit. Also, deeply satisfying personal experiences result from engaging productively with stimulating and interesting people and making new and valuable friendships. Good works do attract good people, and important good works attract the best.

Notes

1. In addition to authoring several good books on how to make money in investing, Claude N. Rosenberg wrote *Wealthy and Wise*, a pioneering book on how to think through what you can afford to give to others. His analysis shows that most people could be much more generous than they seem to realize.
2. Richard I. Kirkland Jr., "Should You Leave It All to the Children?," *Fortune*, September 29, 1986.
3. One of my personal "lightbulbs" lit up while I was enjoying clams at Charley O's restaurant in Rockefeller Center in 1974. Huge black-and-white photographs of movie stars decorated the walls; each had a one-line quote under the picture. The movie star looming over my table was the once very dissolute Tasmanian swashbuckler Errol Flynn. His quote: "Any guy who dies with more than 10 grand has made a mistake." While Flynn surely had other things on his mind, I resolved there and then to avoid the mistake of paying any more than necessary in estate taxes by giving during my lifetime. I prefer to make some errors of *commission* (giving to causes that later disappoint) than to make errors of *omission* (giving too little or too late). It's been interesting and fun—and very rewarding.

CHAPTER 26

THOUGHTS FOR THE WEALTHY

IF YOU ARE SO FORTUNATE AS TO HAVE OVER $20 MILLION, YOU know you have achieved a great success. Congratulations! Fewer than 100,000 Americans have done this well financially. Most likely, you recognize that you have new kinds of problems. How do you find investment advisors and investment managers who are right for you? How much do you pass on to your children and grandchildren—and when do you do it? How much do you commit to philanthropy—and when?

If you have a much larger fortune—over $100 million—you should consider organizing an investment committee or having a personal expert to advise you on all aspects of investing. If paying 1 to 2 percent of assets to an investment advisor year after year seems high to you—as it sure does to me—an alternative is to engage an advisor once every 5 or 10 years on a fee-for-time basis to conduct a thorough evaluation of all your financial and investment plans to be sure they make sense for you. If your personal expert helps save you from just one major mistake or helps you make one wise move, you'll have found a bargain. (*Tip:* some of the best-informed and most thoughtful investment professionals work at large foundations and educational endowments or at large corporate pension funds; they might be glad to help you on weekends for a nice per diem compensation.)

You'll also be wise to retain one of the finest trust and estate lawyers. (*Tip:* young lawyers can be best because they are building their practices and will still be practicing many years from now, so you and your wealth will have continuing service from the same trusted advisor.) Finally, retain the best young partner at a major accounting firm as an advisor and overseer and jointly hire a superb part-time bookkeeper you like personally to maintain all the records, report monthly, and "watch the watchmen" by monitoring investments. (Good bookkeepers who retire often like to work part-time.)

If you have won the "money game," ask yourself: Is it more important for you to concentrate on offense to win even more, or is it better to concentrate on defense and lose less? If you have substantial wealth, you'll be inundated by delightful, articulate people known in the trade as "asset gatherers" because of their ability to win the trust of wealthy people. You may enjoy seeing how personally charming they can be, but please be cautious and check their references carefully.

"Alternative" investments have been in the limelight partly because some practitioners are paid astronomical amounts and make good copy for the media, partly because some have achieved extraordinary investment results, and partly because so many investors still hope to find a way to obtain high returns with little risk.

Another reason alternative investing has attracted so much attention is that it has worked well for four of the earliest, largest, and most skillful practitioners: Yale, Harvard, MIT, and Princeton. (*Full disclosure:* I served as chair of Yale's investment committee for many years.) Their results are extraordinary and, equally important, have been achieved systematically through a rigorously disciplined process. But they are very hard to replicate. Don't even *think* of trying!

When friends on other investment committees repeat that great line from *When Harry Met Sally*—"I'll have what she's having"—I'm reminded of a growing-up experience. When I was eight, our mother took my sister, brother, and me to the Ringling Bros. and Barnum & Bailey Circus. Impressed by the daring young acrobats on the flying trapeze, I resolved to try it at home, with predictable results. I got skinned knees, skinned elbows, and a skinned chin—and learned that copying experts is not easy. (Old Wall Street question: "What's the fastest way to make a small fortune?" Answer: "Start with a large fortune and try to copy the experts.") So here are some friendly warnings about recently popular but unconventional ways to invest.[1]

Hedge Funds

Hedge funds burst on the scene partly because they performed well in the millennium market collapse of dot-com stocks, but primarily because they offer their managers an amazingly powerful way to get rich. The 2 percent fee easily covers all costs of running the fund, plus the manager gets 20 percent of all profits. Learning that smart friends are making $10 million in a single year (and several hedge fund managers made over $1 *billion* in one year) is hard to ignore if you are gifted, young, competitive, and keen to make a fortune yourself *and* want to work in a small shop with several other brilliant people trying to figure things out. It's fun. It's interesting. And when it clicks, you make serious money. Who wouldn't be interested?

Hedge funds come in an almost infinite variety of strategies. They are run by brilliant, intensely striving, supremely confident, fashionably dressed managers with distinguished academic and employment records. However, most hedge funds have a major problem: other hedge funds. As soon as one hedge fund develops an "edge"—a new winning way of investing—other hedge funds try to figure it out so they can use it too. Pretty soon, the edge gets arbitraged down to normal returns and a new edge is needed. Creating edges is hard; creating a series of edges is very hard. That's one of the reasons over 10 percent of hedge funds disappear each year. Meanwhile, the performance records of most hedge funds have been disappointing, largely due to crowding.

The fundamental challenge for hedge funds—and therefore for those investing in hedge funds—is in the numbers. If the rate of return for stocks is 7 percent, the break-even return for a hedge fund has to be 11.25 percent to cover all the fees. This requires "alpha" (the extra return from superior management) of 4.25 percent, which is over 60 percent *more* than the expected *market* return—a *very* large superiority. Some hedge funds will get that high return, and some will get more, but that's not the real question. The real question is whether the fund *you* invest in will do that well year after year—particularly as more money goes into hedge funds that compete with one another in the search to capture alpha.

Venture Capital

Venture capital attracts attention. Over the long term, the surging flow of investment capital into venture capital funds has been astonishing. No doubt there is romance about discovering explosively successful companies like Apple, eBay, Facebook, Google, or Uber and making more than 100 times your investment. But before investing in venture capital, consider the following: over the past 30 years, while the median return of the top quartile of venture capital funds was 28 percent, the median return of *all* venture capital funds was actually less than 5 percent (that is, less than the returns on Treasury bonds). The 10 most successful venture capital investment organizations made combined profits higher than the total "excess returns" (returns over and above

those of the S&P 500 index) of the entire venture capital industry. In other words, relative to the overall market, all the other
funds collectively *lost* money, gave up liquidity, and took serious
risk. The leading venture capital firms are continually the leaders—for strong reasons—and the odds are high that they will
continue to be the most successful.

The secret to success in venture capital is no secret. It's *not* the
money. Money to invest is necessary but not nearly sufficient. And
the best venture capital managers are not simply shrewd backers
of exciting new products. They are good at this, of course, but
their great strengths are two: they know how to select entrepreneurs, and they know how to help bring effective teams together
to build unusually successful companies. They are certainly *not*
passive investors; they are vigorously active and creative. Savvy
budding entrepreneurs learn from already successful entrepreneurs how important the best venture investors can be in helping
their new companies succeed. So the best entrepreneurs with the
best ideas all want to work with the best venture investors.

The best venture investors are always in touch with the large,
medium, and small companies in the industries they plan to
invest in. They make sure that the most exciting young stars
who might decide to launch new companies know how important their assistance can be and how often they have made crucial
differences to the fledgling companies they've invested in. Specializing in specific aspects of technology, they know all the
most effective engineers, salespeople, production managers,
and financial experts. They know why these people are so effective, and they appreciate how particular people can fit together
as successful teams. They use this expertise to help their companies get smarter and stronger and become much more likely
to succeed. And they know that effective entrepreneurs almost
always change their products, business plans, and target markets as they learn what works and what doesn't work. They
don't fixate on products or markets or business plans—no matter

how exciting—because they know the key to success is always the entrepreneur who has a compelling need to succeed *and* is a skillful risk manager (*not* a risk-taker).

It's no accident that the winners keep winning. There's only one problem: you cannot use this insight. Like the best hedge funds, the best venture capital organizations are closed to new investors. In fact, they are already overbooked and unable to accommodate all the money that even their long-standing investor clients want to give them. In addition, some of their successful entrepreneurs now have large amounts they'd like to invest. And the venture managers, having made large fortunes in successful past investments, want to invest more of their own money. Long story short: you can't get into the funds you'd want to invest in. The other venture funds remind wise investors of Groucho Marx's sardonic remark: "I don't care to belong to any club that will accept people like me as a member."

Real Estate

Real estate has many appeals. A remarkable proportion of the nation's wealthiest individuals and families made their fortunes in real estate. Tax advantages are a major factor; astute use of leverage and access to credit—lots of it—are important; exceptional skill at adversarial negotiations is crucial; patience and decisive action are both essential. In addition, success depends on extraordinary, intimate knowledge of all the relevant details of each local market and, within a chosen market, of each property, its tenants, and their lease agreements; clever insights into ways specific improvements will significantly enhance future rentals; and a special ability to attract desirable tenants. An absolute devotion to the business is mandatory.

Few people would be willing and able to meet all these requirements, and hardly anybody can hope to succeed on a part-time basis. That's why those who do devote themselves to real estate investing can, if fortune smiles on them, do so very well.

If you want to invest in real estate without a big time commitment, you can invest in the common stocks of REITs (real estate investment trusts), which are listed on the principal exchanges. They trade at prices reflecting both real estate and the overall stock market, with long-term returns similar to overall stock returns.

Private Equity

As with other specialized alternative investments, the best private equity funds are closed to new investors. That's okay for individual investors because private equity funds—overall and on average—have *under*performed the market averages after their substantial leverage was factored in. In other words, investors would be better off *and* have more liquidity by buying publicly traded stocks with moderate "margin" debt.

Commodities

Commodities are economically inert and so do not develop increasing economic value. Changes in their prices are driven only by changes in demand or supply. Those who buy and sell commodities are not investing; they are speculating that they know more or better than the market. They may be right with their bets and trades, but for every right there must always be an equal wrong. The total of all trading adds up to a negative—a zero-sum game minus the costs of trading. Gold has attracted attention in recent years, particularly since the creation of gold ETFs. Gold has changed in price, and bulls predict a higher price. But investors will want to remember that the inflation-adjusted price of gold in early 1980 was over $2,250 an ounce.

Note

1. Great success is usually achieved through specialization in one line of work or one kind of investing. However, most financially successful people will be wise to be defensive in the diversification of their investments. If you have won the money game, it makes no sense to risk converting a win into a loss by trying too hard.

CHAPTER 27

YOU ARE NOW
GOOD TO GO!

YOU—NOT YOUR INVESTMENT MANAGERS—HAVE THE MOST important job in successful investment management. Your central responsibilities are to decide on your long-term investment objectives and determine a reasoned and realistic set of investment policies that can achieve your objectives—with or without the help of a professional investment advisor.

You should study your total investment situation, your emotional tolerance for risk, the history of investment markets, and how they would interplay, because a mismatch between the market's sometimes grim realities and your financial and emotional needs can result—and as recently as 2008 did result—in great harm.

Investors who study past realities of investing will be able to protect themselves and their investments from the all too common and unrealistic belief that they can find active managers who will substantially beat the market by beating the expert competition. If the question were "Can we find a team of brilliant, well-informed, hardworking, and experienced managers who would do their very best?" the answer would be a resounding "Yes!" But that would be the wrong question. The right question would be, "Can we find an investment manager who can outperform the consensus of experts by enough to cover fees and costs and offset the risks and uncertainties?"

The well-informed investor understands that the only way an active investment manager can beat the market is to find and exploit other investors' mistakes more often than they find and exploit his or her mistakes. This investor understands that a manager who strives to beat the market is all too likely to try too hard and get beaten instead. Most of the clients who insist on trying—either on their own or with professional managers—will be disappointed by the results. Active investing *is* a loser's game.

Happily, there is an easy way to win the loser's game, simply by *not* playing by the historical conventions, which, given the many major changes, are now seriously out of date. Raised in the tradition that says, "If you find a problem, find a solution," I felt intrigued by the task of finding a solution to the problem identified more than 40 years ago in my article "The Loser's Game."[1] As is so often true, the solution was to "think outside the box" and redefine the problem. Thus, the focus shifted from the loser's game (working ever harder in a futile effort to beat the experts' market) to the winner's game of concentrating on the big picture of your longer-term objectives, asset mix, and investment policies—and staying the course.

Individual investors are important for three major reasons. First, there are so many: nearly 50 million in the United States and an equal number in other nations. Second, most individual investors are truly on their own in designing long-term investment policies and strategies (even though investment consultants can provide the counseling most individuals need for a reasonable hourly fee). Third, most "how-to" books on investing are sold on the false promise that the typical individual can beat the market concerns of professional investors. He can't, and she won't.

Fortunately, the individual investor does not have to beat the market to be successful. Attempting to beat the market will distract you from the important, interesting, and highly productive task of designing a realistic long-term investing program that will succeed at providing the results best for you.

Soundly conceived, persistently followed long-term investment policies are the pathway to success in investing. The actions required are not complicated. If you feel, as I do, that some of the advice in this book is pretty simple, remember Warren Buffett's wonderful summary: "Investing *is* simple—but it's not easy."[2] The real challenge is to commit to the discipline of long-term investing and avoid reacting to Mr. Market's compelling distractions, which are superfluous to the real work of investing. A persistent commitment to the discipline of long-term investing is your principal responsibility *and* your best opportunity to assure your own long-term investing success.

There are two different kinds of problems in trying to beat the market. One problem is that this is extraordinarily difficult to do, and it's all too easy, while trying to do better, to do *worse*— even much worse. The other problem is that it will divert your attention from establishing long-range objectives and investment policies that are well matched to your particular needs.

Winning the loser's game of beating the market is easy: *Do not play it.* Concentrate on the winner's game of defining and adhering faithfully to sound investment policies that are right for the market realities and right for your long-term goals and objectives that you can sustain.

The needs and purposes of different investors are not the same, so their investment portfolios should not be the same. You have already answered the important questions: Where are you and who are you financially? How long will the money be invested? What are your assets, income, debts, and responsibilities? How do you feel about market risk? Can you trust yourself to be a persistent long-term investor? The answers to these few questions are what make each of us unique as investors.

To fulfill your financial responsibilities to yourself, you need three characteristics:

1. A genuine interest in developing an understanding of your own true values and investment objectives.
2. A basic appreciation of the fundamental nature of capital markets and investments, including Mr. Market's clever tricks and the market dominance of powerful institutional investors.
3. The personal discipline to work out and hold on to the basic policies that will, over time, succeed in fulfilling your realistic investment objectives. That's what this book is all about.

While this book is a spirited critique of contemporary investment practice, it is by no means a condemnation of investment managers. The problem is not that professional managers lack skill or diligence. Quite the opposite. The problem with trying to beat the market is that so many professional investors are so talented and so dedicated to their work *and* all have equal instant access to so much superb information and competing power that, as a highly competitive group, they make it very difficult for any one of their number—and virtually impossible for most investors—to do better, particularly in the long run.

This book is written with a clear point of view: the real purpose of investment management is *not* to beat the market; it is to do what is right for each particular investor who accepts the central responsibility of defining his or her true and realistic investment objectives, developing sensible long-term policies, *and* staying with them. Much as it might seem obvious that investors should care a lot about the way their money is managed, the reality is that they typically do too little—until it's too late. This book is written for investors who are prepared to take charge of their own investment destiny.

Professional investment advisors should encourage their clients to use this book as a guide to performing the vital role of being informed, active, and therefore *successful* clients.

When you have finished digesting the straightforward propositions presented in this short book, you will know all you will ever need to know to be truly successful with investments. You are now ready to enjoy *winning investing*. You're good to go!

Notes

1. Written in 1975 for the *Financial Analysts Journal*, the article won the profession's Graham and Dodd Award.
2. Two of my friends, at the peak of their distinguished careers in medicine and medical research, agree that the two most important discoveries in medical history were penicillin and the importance of hand washing (which stopped the spreading of infection from one mother to another via the midwives who delivered most babies before 1900). What's more, my friends counsel, there's no better advice on how to live longer and healthier lives than to quit smoking and buckle up when driving. The lesson: advice doesn't have to be complicated to be good.

CHAPTER 28

PARTING THOUGHTS

G ENUINE DOUBT, SAID THE PHYSICIST RICHARD FEYNMAN, IS the necessary first step toward creativity. So I've learned to double-check my answers, particularly when the evidence seems most confirming, and to ask, "Could I be wrong?" On the main parts of my argument, I've checked with experts over many years and am confident that certain basic structural realities are not going to change:

- The number of brilliant, hardworking investment profession-als is not going to decrease enough to convert active investing back into the winner's game of the 1960s, 1970s, and 1980s.
- The proportion of transactions made by institutions—and the splendid professionals who lead them—will not decline. Investing, therefore, will stay dangerous for even the most gifted amateur.
- Maybe someday so many investors will have agreed to index that the "last stock pickers standing" will have the field all to themselves. *That'll* be the day! Meanwhile, I've got better things to do, and so do you—we can play to win with both our time and our money by focusing on determining the asset mix policy best suited to our true objectives..

SERVING ON INVESTMENT COMMITTEES

INSTITUTIONAL INVESTING IS VERY DIFFERENT FROM INDIVIDUAL investing, and that's not just because, to cite Hemingway's classic retort to F. Scott Fitzgerald, "Yes, they have more money." Many of us have the opportunity to serve on the investment committees of endowments, pension funds, or other institutions, and all who serve want to be helpful. Here is a primer on what to expect and how to be most helpful.

Most institutional funds are perpetual or nearly perpetual and are governed by committees that delegate investing to external managers. The investment committee's primary responsibility is not investment *management* but to assure good *governance*.

For most investment committees, the main task and responsibility is determining the appropriate goals for both interim market risk and long-term returns and then deciding on the long-term investment policies that will best achieve those goals and bring harmony to the complementary disciplines of investing and managing the institution's finances. After that comes ensuring that effective working relationships are developed with investment managers. (As explained in earlier chapters,

increasing numbers of institutions are investing larger percentages in index funds. This decision to index is wise *and* makes
"partnering" easy.)

At multibillion-dollar funds, the important work of managing
managers will be handled by a full-time staff and overseen by
the investment committee. But for most funds under $1 billion,
the manager management decisions are made by the investment
committee itself.

As in any good business relationship, the responsibilities and
undertakings of each party—the client and the investment manager—should be realistic and clear to both. In particular, the
investment manager's mission should be explicit, in writing,
mutually agreed upon, and reaffirmed (or modified) once each
year. The mission should clearly be within the manager's competence and realistic relative to the market.

The relationship between client and manager will usually be
centered on regular meetings organized to achieve together the
success that is desired by both the investment manager and the
investment committee. Every meeting should be designed and
controlled by the client—*not* by the manager, as so often happens. The committee chair should establish the agenda, and the
investment manager should furnish all relevant documentation
for the meeting, allowing ample time for careful preparation by
the members of the committee. The emphasis on *relevant* documentation is deliberate; it takes little genius to flood a meeting
with enough statistical trivia to obfuscate the central issues.

Long-term investment policies should be clearly separated
from investment operations because they are very different
responsibilities. Only by separating portfolio operations from
policy formation can responsibility and accountability be established for each of these two different but complementary aspects
of investment management. Of course, investment policy and
investment operations are not kept in isolation from each other.
Operating performance should be evaluated objectively to be

sure operations are in accord with policy, and investment policies should be evaluated objectively against long-term returns to be sure that the policies are realistic and effective. All too often, responsibility for investment policy is delegated to fund managers along with the operating management of the portfolio. Mixing investment policy and portfolio operations—problem definition and problem solving—and then delegating both is asking for trouble.

The specialized language derived from modern portfolio theory makes it relatively easy to specify investment objectives and policies. Sharpe ratios (a measure of excess returns relative to risk) and benchmark returns allow clients to monitor how well portfolio operations conform to agreed-upon policy. This information enables each portfolio manager to achieve good performance—*not* by heroically "beating the market" but by faithfully and sensibly carrying out realistic investment policies to achieve well-defined objectives.

The investment committee and its investment managers should agree explicitly on each of these important policy dimensions:

1. The level of market risk to be taken by the portfolio.
2. Whether the level of risk is to be sustained or varied as markets change.
3. Whether individual stock risk or market segment risk is to be taken or avoided *and* the incremental rate of return that such risks, when taken, are expected to produce for the portfolio.

As active managers are given more and more discretion to deviate from a market-matching index fund and take more and different kinds of risks—market risk, stock-group risk, and individual-stock risk—the difficulty of determining how much of any specific period's portfolio return is the result of skill, as opposed to chance, increases rapidly.

The operational performance of the investment manager should be measured and evaluated by direct comparison with explicit investment policies—and only by comparison with explicit policies. For example, it would be both unfair and misleading to attempt to evaluate the operational performance of a portfolio of growth stocks or small cap stocks by comparing results with overall market averages. (All too often, a growth specialist or a small cap specialist will be cheered *or* jeered—equally unfairly—when that specialty just happens to be in favor *or* out of favor in the overall market.)[1]

Each meeting with an investment manager should begin with a brief review of the manager's agreed-upon mission to see if any modification in objective or policy is appropriate. If neither the client nor the investment manager has any changes in the investment mission to propose, both should explicitly reaffirm the mission statement.

If either the client or the manager wishes to propose a change, the proposed change and the rationale supporting it should be prepared in advance and distributed as one of the meeting preparation documents so all participants can study and think through the proposed change well before the meeting. There should be no surprises in this most important part of the meeting.

Discussion of specific portfolio operations—purchases and sales of specific securities—should be made only on an exception basis and should be brief. This portion of the meeting should *not* be "interesting." Clients should not accept colorful war stories or capsule reviews of specific stocks. These *are* fun, but they are entertainment, not enlightenment. Instead, this part of the meeting should be a straightforward confirmation that the manager has sensibly and faithfully followed agreed-upon policy. Ideally, the review of operations and reaffirmation of the investment manager's mission should take just five minutes. If they take longer, "Houston, we have a problem." Something is wrong: either the mission is not clear, or the results are off mission.

The balance of the meeting time, usually about an hour, can best be devoted to a thoughtful and detailed discussion of any one or two of the many topics of importance to both the client and the manager, as a way of increasing shared understanding of the active manager's investing concept and process. Discussion topics could include a significant economic development that affects portfolio strategy, research supporting a major portfolio commitment, or the changing investment attraction of a particular industry. The important purpose of these topical discussions is to enable the investment committee to take a deeper look into the thinking process of the investment manager.

If portfolio operations have not been in accord with agreed-upon policy and the investment manager's agreed-upon mission, it is not really important whether current portfolio results happen to be above (lucky you) or below (unlucky you) the results that would be expected if the policy had been followed faithfully. In either case, the truly important information is that the portfolio and the portfolio manager are out of conformance and probably somewhat out of control. Sooner or later, this lack of control will show up in losses—all too often, unrecoverable losses.

The main reason for measuring performance is to improve client-manager communication. The purpose of performance measurement is not to provide *answers* but to identify *questions* that investors and managers should explore together to be sure they have a good mutual understanding of what is contributing to and what is detracting from investment performance. Ask the child's favorite series of questions: Why? Why? Why? Committee members may find that just one or two decisions—perhaps brilliantly skillful, perhaps lucky, perhaps both—can make a powerful difference in the reported performance of an active manager.

The final area of performance evaluation is clearly qualitative. Does the active manager's explanation of his or her decisions make good sense? Are the active manager's actions consistent with his or her words at the previous meeting? As a thoughtful, interested client, do you find your confidence in the manager's abilities, knowledge, and judgment rising as you have more and more discussions—or falling? Committee members should give real weight to these "soft" qualitative factors because, over and over again, this is where the best signals of real trouble first surface, long before the problem is evident in hard quantitative data.

At least once a year, there should be a candid review of your institution's overall financial situation—the context in which the investment portfolio fits. Similarly, the investment manager should devote part of one meeting each year to a discussion of his or her organization's professional and business development, with particular emphasis on long-term policies and commitments to strengthen professional capabilities.

Meetings should *not* be used—as they almost always are—for a brief and ultimately meaningless tour of the investment world that might include superficial comments on the economic outlook, recent changes in interest rates, a review of minor changes in the weightings of industry groups in the equity portfolio, and a quick recap of modest shifts in quality ratings in the bond portfolio, concluding with some "interesting" insights into a few specific decisions. Without really digging into any of the major decisions made, this will use up time that otherwise might be devoted to serious discussions of subjects of potentially enduring importance to the portfolio—and to a successful long-term relationship.

A written summary of key points, facts, and views expressed— in three to five pages—should be prepared and distributed after each meeting and kept for future use and reference. One good suggestion would be for the client and the investment manager to alternate writing these meeting summaries.

Investment committees that do not have professional staffs— and not having a savvy staff certainly strengthens the case for indexing—have four levels of operational decisions to make.

First, should a manager be changed? The normal expectation is no. Second, if any manager is identified as "up for review," there should be a rigorous analysis of the cases for and against taking action. Give particular care and attention to the case for *not* taking action. Experience shows that the best decision is often the counterintuitive one: to assign *more* money to the manager who has been recently *under*performing. Reason: the well-chosen active manager will probably be underperforming only because his or her style is temporarily out of favor in the market and probably will outperform again when market conditions are more favorable to his or her style. Committees all too often drop managers they should keep and switch to managers who have just finished their best periods. The transaction costs of making these changes are high, particularly when the terminated manager goes on to do well and the newly hired manager has already peaked and will underperform after being chosen.

Third, should the terms or size of assets being managed by any continuing manager be changed or modified in any significant way?

Fourth, should the long-term policy on asset mix be changed? If not, would a significant temporary deviation be appropriate? If not, the formal part of the meeting is over.

In this format, decisions are made on an exception basis. Decisions to act are few and far between because you already will have done the homework rigorously, will know your true objectives, and will have decided on sensible long-term investment policy *and* on the specific mission for each manager. Having made decisions for the long term, you should need to make few, if any, changes.

How long should an ideal meeting take? Actually, about five minutes—with no actions taken because no actions are needed. As every experienced manager of continuous-process factories knows, one indication of a well-run continuous process, such as investment management should strive to be, is that nothing "interesting" is going on because anything interesting is a problem. A well-run continuous-process plant—and investment management is a *very* long-term continuous process—is problem free and does not need corrections.

Here are some of the questions investment committees might ask prospective investment managers and pursue to a full understanding:

- How have your investment management concepts and process changed over the past decade? Why? How might they change in the *next* decade?
- How have you changed your professional organization over the past decade to increase your professional capability and capacity to manage assets?
- How have you changed your business strategy in the past? How might you change it in the future? Why?
- What is your plan for leadership development and succession?
- What is the compensation of your senior professional and business leaders, and how is it determined?

Keep notes on the answers your investment manager gives to your questions for future use in comparing the answers you will get at other times to the same or similar questions. (Because it works so well, this simple technique has been used for years, perhaps even for centuries, by the managers of the Scottish investment trusts and by the Japanese.)

If and when you decide to terminate an investment manager, do yourself a favor and recognize that the failure may not be the manager's; it may be yours. So don't go looking for a new manager until you've taken the time and care to learn how you could do a better job of selecting and working with each of your managers.

Because index funds are readily available at a low cost, the use of multiple active managers cannot be justified as a way to diversify a public securities portfolio and reduce risk. That can be accomplished much more easily and cheaply with a simple, broad market index fund.

Whatever spending rule is adopted for an endowment, two cardinal principles should govern: the rule should be set at a level that will be sustained through major bull and bear markets, and the difference between rate of return and spending—that is, the amount that gets reinvested in the endowment—should be enough to absorb fully the corrosive powers of inflation.

A pension fund's actuarial rate of return assumption or an endowment's spending rule should be determined by investment results, not the other way around. Trustees should never let spending wishes or "needs" determine investment management practices or policies.

By clearly separating the work of management from the work of governance, best-practice investment committees demonstrate that they understand that good governance provides the long-term policy framework and ensures the working environment that helps operating managers to do their work both efficiently and effectively.

Who should serve on a best-practice investment committee? The organization's chief executive or chief financial officer, most particularly, should always serve on or meet regularly with the investment committee to make sure the committee understands the organization's financial management challenges—near and long term. Investment committees need thoughtful and informed members ready and able to make judgments based on the kind of wisdom that can only come from experience in investing, so a large majority of the members of each investment committee should have substantial experience as investors. A minority of committee members may be chosen for other reasons, such as understanding of the institution and its finances. All members should have demonstrated good judgment of people, concepts, and organizations—and should "play well with others."

Service on committees should be staggered and planned. Terms of five or six years—renewable once or even twice—help committees remove quietly those who are not effective or not enjoying service. Members should differ in background, experience, and skills. Tenure on best-practice committees should *average* six to eight years. (For effectiveness in all sorts of working groups, this average proves to be optimal. Shorter average tenure often means that members are too new to one another to know how to be great "co-listeners" and work as a true team. Longer average tenure can mean that members have stopped listening carefully to one another.)

Investment committees—usually meeting four times each year—have two reasons for concentrating on governance and not attempting management. First, in today's fast-changing capital markets, committees meeting quarterly are ill suited to making operational decisions. They just can't do it well. Second, even the best-organized and best-led committees will find themselves fully challenged by the responsibilities of good governance: setting appropriate limits on risk, setting optimal investment policies and objectives, agreeing on portfolio structure, ensuring wise selection of investment managers, staying on a steady course during periods of market euphoria and market anxieties and fears, formulating sensible spending rules, and coordinating with the finance committee and the full board of trustees so that the endowment performs its full and appropriate role in the overall fiscal governance of the institution.

While all investment committees are, of course, interested in good long-term rates of return, the best practitioners know that their first priority must always be managing risks, particularly in buoyant times, when risks are easily overlooked.

The expected duration of each manager relationship should be very long—ideally, *forever.* Forever may seem an unrealistically long time. It's not. The cost of changing managers for high-turnover funds can be far greater than the 3 to 5 percent transaction costs usually cited. Add to these costs the hidden costs of distracting the committee and management from working rigorously on their real responsibility of developing superb working relationships with their best managers. While committees all blame turnover on the managers, the real culprits are often the committees that hire impatiently—sometimes after only a one-hour "speed dating" presentation. Then, because the main consideration is "good performance" versus the market, they repeat the in-and-out, in-and-out sequence, increasing the frustrations of both managers and committee members. Both know there must be a better way.

The obvious advantage of indexing is lower fees and costs, but that's not as important over the long run as the better investment results. And those better results are not nearly as important as this: indexing keeps the committee focused on what really matters—getting it right on the asset mix and long-term investment policies.

A final word: serving on an investment committee should be interesting, enjoyable, and fulfilling. If your committee does not measure up on all three criteria, change it. If you really can't change it, resign—and serve elsewhere. Best-practice committees are designed to be successful in all three dimensions. There's no reason not to be on a best-practice investment committee. Sure, organizing such a committee takes thoughtful leadership, but it's also much more fun.

Note

1. The classic example of how hard it is to use performance data correctly was the impact on American Research & Development Corporation, a venture capital fund, of a spectacularly successful, but small and almost accidental investment in Digital Equipment Corporation in 1967. AR&D decided, just

barely, that it had an obligation to an MIT professor who thought he had been promised financial support to launch the company. With the Digital investment, AR&D outperformed the market averages. Without Digital, AR&D would have underperformed the market over its 20-year life.

MURDER ON
THE ORIENT EXPRESS

GATHA CHRISTIE—FOR MANY YEARS THE WORLD'S FAVORITE mystery writer[1]—perfected her guessing game for readers by creating a marvelous "Can you solve it?" puzzle in *Murder on the Orient Express*. Clues pointed in many directions but gave no certainty. Eventually, the plot thickened and Hercule Poirot, the wily Belgian investigator, deftly guided readers to an eventually obvious conclusion: no *one* suspect was guilty—*all* the suspects were guilty.

The same reality may explain the persistent failure of mutual funds and other institutional investors to achieve their ubiquitous but evanescent investment goal of superior results, or "beat the market" performance. The results are persistently disappointing, clues to the causes and leads to suspects abound, and suspicions and evidence indicate a full array of possible culprits, any one of whom may be the perpetrator.

However unintentionally, the "failure to perform" problem is made even worse by many investors aiming very high and setting inherently unrealistic expectations and then taking on high volatility managers because their recent performance looks better. Despite the obvious statistical impossibility of more than one in four achieving top-quartile results, a majority of funds—obviously more than twice the top-quartile objective capacity—solemnly declare this as their objective. *Lake Wobegon* fans would not be surprised. Nor would behavioral economists, whose research shows the famous 80:20 rule at work in many self-evaluations. About 80 percent of the folks in one group after another rate themselves "above average" as friends, as conversationalists, as drivers, or as dancers, as well as in having a good sense of humor, good judgment, and being trustworthy.

Maybe it's just human nature to be qualitatively optimistic about ourselves. But investment results can always be subjected to objective analysis. Extensive and readily available data show that in a random 12-month period, about 60 percent of mutual fund managers underperform; lengthen the time period to 10 years, and the proportion that fails to perform rises above 70 percent; and while the data are not robust for 20-year time periods, the proportion falling behind the market for this longer period is over 80 percent.

At least as concerning, equity managers who underperform do so by one and a half times as much as outperforming funds beat their chosen benchmarks—so the funds' "slugging average" is doubly daunting. Research on the performance of institutional portfolios shows that after risk adjustment 24 percent of funds fall significantly short of their chosen market benchmarks and have negative alpha, 75 percent of funds roughly match the market—have zero alpha—and less than 1 percent achieve statistically significantly superior results after costs, a number not much different from zero.[2] So let's look at the evidence to see why institutional funds have been underperforming.

Data from more than 35 years of research on the specific managers used by institutional funds show that large numbers of new accounts go to managers who have produced superior recent results—mostly *after* these managers' best performance years—and away from underperforming managers *after* their worst performance years. (Another oft-repeated negative factor is moving into asset classes or subclasses *after* prices have risen and out of asset classes or subclasses *after* prices have fallen—moving assets in the wrong direction at the wrong time.) This "buy high, sell low" pattern of behavior burdens investors with billions of dollars in costs.[3] Forensic evidence in Figure B.1 shows that institutional investors—despite their many competitive advantages, including full-time staff, consultants, and ability to select those they consider the very best managers—typically underperform their chosen benchmarks.

Figure B.1 Before-and-after excess returns for fired and hired investment managers

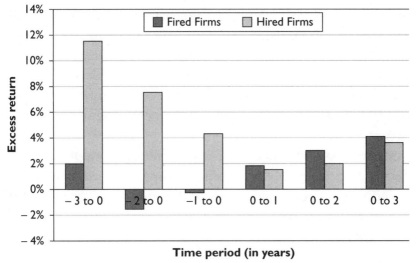

Source: *Goyal and Wahal, 2008. The Journal of Finance. Vol. LXIII, No. 4. August 2008.*

Note: All of the differences between fired and hired managers before the firing are significant. The differences between fired and hired managers after the change are not statistically significant.

In a recent study of more than 3,000 institutional funds, the managers who were to be hired had achieved—over the three years *before* their hiring—significantly higher returns than the managers who were to be fired.[4] (The to-be-hired managers produced substantial excess returns on domestic equities of 12.5 percent, 7.8 percent, and 4.3 percent annually over three years.)

However, for the three years after the new managers were hired, the fired managers actually achieved slightly higher returns than the new managers.

This difference—repeated over and over—incurs two kinds of costs that accumulate through repetition. Significantly, what matters most is not the trivial cost of the underperformance of the new manager versus the fired manager *after* the change, but the substantial underperformance of the soon-to-be-fired managers over the years *before* the change.

Ironically, once the hiring has been done, almost nobody involved studies how often or why the process of hiring managers later disappoints. Terminated active managers may tell themselves that their poor runs were just temporary "anomalies" and with unsubstantiated optimism look forward to better times and, they hope, better results. Meanwhile, clients tell themselves that they were wise to get rid of the bad managers. If neither clients nor managers examine or learn from their actual experience, the problem of persistent underperformance will surely continue.[5]

If clients did examine their experience, they would see that the most serious cost comes from the risks they had taken when trying to identify managers who *might* produce superior performance. But using past performance to identify which managers are likely to achieve superior future performance will increase the odds of disappointment, because past performance—however compelling it may appear—does not predict future performance.

A specter is stalking active management. The very small "commodity" fees charged for index funds[6] that consistently provide market-matching returns at market-matching risk mean that active managers can only hope to deliver real value when they beat the market—which, we now know, most do not do, particularly over the long term. True fees—*incremental* fees as a percentage of *incremental* value added—are actually over 100 percent of the value delivered by active managers.

As explained in Chapter 21, the real marginal cost of active management is the incremental fee active managers charge versus the incremental returns they deliver.[7] Seen correctly, active management may be the only service ever offered that costs more than the value delivered. (Students of real versus apparent cost will remind us that the true cost of a puppy is not the purchase price, nor the payment to the boat broker the true cost of a yacht. On the latter, J. P. Morgan famously observed, "If you have to ask what it costs, you cannot afford it.")

Increasingly, clients are realizing that fees are a major part of the problem of underperformance—particularly in today's highly professionalized market. The cruel irony is that so many active managers are so skillful, hardworking, and capable that they collectively dominate the market. So few, if any, can beat the expert consensus *and*, disconcertingly, investors cannot tell which ones will.

The investment profession is not lacking in possible suspects for the crime of systemic underperformance. After three decades of working on business strategy with major investment management firms in Europe, Asia, and all over North America, I came to the realization that the prime suspects *had* to be investment managers.

The circumstantial evidence was substantial. Active managers—knowing they are talented, hardworking, well trained, and dedicated—believe deeply in the value of their work. (Behavioral economists call this *familiarity bias*.) Almost every active manager gave in to the understandable temptation during new business presentations *and* in quarterly review meetings to present their performance records in the most favorable light. So their records were almost always "enhanced."[8] The years included in historical performance charts were often chosen to make the best impression, and the benchmarks against which results were compared were often selected for similar reasons.

Another clue: investment philosophies and decision-making processes—no matter how complex they might have been to implement—were all too often oversimplified, documented with selected data, and crisply articulated as convincing "universal truths." Prospects and clients were led to believe that each manager had developed a compelling conceptual competitive advantage in the battle for performance. No manager talked candidly about how difficult investment management had become as company information and rigorous analyses proliferated, competitors multiplied, and information once seen as the "secret sauce"—an active manager's competitive advantage—had gotten increasingly commoditized.

Realists would suspect that as much as investment managers might have wanted to build their firms on the basis of superior performance, the more compelling motivation had become economic: to win more new business and keep as much old business as possible. After nearly three decades of behind-the-scenes experience with more than 200 investment organizations of many sizes in several nations, my view was increasingly drawn toward the suspicions of the realists. A close examination of the competitive rankings of investment managers made a compelling case: over and over again—even when they had to know that in the future it would be terribly hard to continue producing recently achieved superior results—managers made special efforts to go out and sell their services and win new accounts when their recent years' performance numbers were particularly favorable. Well, they would, wouldn't they?[9] Realists recognized that those managers who sold hard to get new business when their results looked best *won* more business and those that temporized skillfully during patches of underperformance *kept* more. So if observers were asked, "Whodunit?" the evidence pointed to the investment managers being guilty of causing institutional underperformance.

On reflection, however, I realized that another group of suspects had to be considered: investment consultants. They are paid to monitor an investor's current managers and help select new managers—after, of course, first helping clients decide to terminate underperforming managers. In the view of most busy investors, it has made sense to use an expert who specializes in evaluating hundreds of potential investment managers, systematically assessing their "performance" numbers, regularly meeting with their key people, and rigorously comparing actual behavior with past promises. These experts, ostensibly dedicated solely to their clients' best interests, are able to do extensive and intensive evaluation, *and* they are independent.

A realist would note that investment consulting is a business. Although consultants would like to achieve great results for their clients, business economics almost inevitably dominate aspirations toward professionalism. Once the research costs of evaluating managers and compiling the database are covered at an investment consulting firm, the annual profitability of an incremental account is over 90 percent. And because well-managed relationships continue for many years into the future, their economic value is not this year's fee but the net present value of many years of future fees. Equally, more than 90 percent of the net present value of any *lost* account's fees is a direct reduction of the controlling firm's profits. So the owners of consulting firms pay close attention to their firms' business relationships, and the priority of every on-the-line manager is clear: do not lose an account. Eventually, this priority inevitably comes to dominate the behavior of everyone in every consulting firm.

Given the great difficulty of the task, it would be naive to assume that any firm could somehow consistently identify managers with superior future capabilities *and* skillfully terminate those who are about to disappoint. It would be far smarter business strategy to build a strong defensive position by encouraging each client to diversify across multiple managers. "The more the merrier" diversification protects the advisor's business by diversifying against the risk of any particular manager's performance difficulties doing harm to the advisor's relationship with his or her client—and to future fees.

An advisor's agency interests are economically focused on keeping the largest number of accounts for as many years as possible. These *agency* interests are not well aligned with the long-term *principal* interests of the client. Though neither party wants it to be that way, a conflict of agency versus principal behavior should have been anticipated.

Of course, I saw that this portfolio diversification strategy led to clients having more managers, which increased the chances of one or more managers producing disappointing results. It also made the investor all the more dependent on the advisor monitoring those managers, plus the managers who might be brought in when one of the current managers faltered or failed. Monitoring all those managers made the investor rely on the advisor for information and evaluations.

Investment advisors learned to present for final selection by the investor only those managers with compelling recent performance records and not to lose points by defending a "disappointing" manager. (Has *any* consultant ever presented an investment manager with the words, "While this manager's recent performance record certainly does not *look* favorable, my professional opinion is that this manager has a particularly strong team and has weathered storms in a market that was not hospitable to its style, which we now believe will achieve superior results in the future"?)

Finally, after tracking which managers win accounts and which lose accounts each year, the record indicates that advisors' clients have been hiring managers *after* their best years and terminating managers *after* their worst years. So the evidence points to this conclusion: The advisors did it! They are guilty of, or at least accomplices in, the crime of causing investors to underperform.

For the careful observer, however, suspicion points in yet another direction: the individual investor or the institutions' fund executives. Investment managers learned long ago always to be represented by socially dominant people who are highly skilled at and paid handsomely for closing transactions and who have an absolute determination to win.[10] Through no fault of their own, institutional fund executives and individual investors are set up to be overwhelmed. Rather than carefully *buying* investment services, most investors are *sold* those services. And the easiest time to get sold on an active investment manager is at the peak of investment performance. So a realist would be drawn, however reluctantly, to the grim conclusion that it's the investors who "dunnit."

But not so fast: Having served with over a dozen investment committees in Asia, North America, Europe, and the Middle East with funds ranging in size all the way from $10 million to $400 billion, I've seen that the evidence points with remarkable consistency at yet another surprising culprit. Despite all their best intentions— both individually and collectively—the perpetrators of the crime of underperformance may well be the investment committees.

Consider the evidence. First, many committees are operating in ways that do not reflect the substantial changes in investment markets that have made obsolete many of the traditional beliefs about investing—particularly those outdated beliefs often still held by the senior people who frequently serve on investment committees. However unintentionally, many investment committees have misdefined their objectives and are organized in ways that are now counterproductive. So, as Shakespeare put it, "The fault, dear Brutus, lies not in our stars, but in ourselves."

But no matter how tempted investment committee members may be to confess—after objectively examining the accumulating evidence—to causing underperformance, committees are not entirely responsible. They *are* guilty, but they are not alone. They have many accomplices. Active investment managers and investment advisors and consultants are also guilty. No *one* suspect is guilty; they are *all* guilty.

In the "end of story" ironic twist so often enjoyed by Agatha Christie's many readers, none of the guilty parties is ready to recognize its own role in the crime of underperformance. All the suspects know they are working conscientiously, know they are working hard, and believe sincerely in their own innocence. They do not recognize their own roles in the crime. Nobody even seems to recognize that a crime has been committed—nor to realize that until they examine the evidence and recognize their own active roles, however unintentionally performed, the crime of active management's underperformance will continue to be committed.

Notes

1. Collectively, Ms. Christie's 66 detective novels and 14 collections of short stories have outsold all but the Bible and Shakespeare.
2. See Laurent Barras, Olivier Scaillet, and Russ Wermers, "False Discoveries in Mutual Fund Performance: Measuring Luck in Estimated Alphas," *Journal of Finance* 65, no. 1 (February 2010): 179–216.
3. See Scott D. Stewart, John J. Neumann, Christopher R. Knittel, and Jeffrey Heisler, "Absence of Value: An Analysis of Investment Allocation Decisions by Institutional Plan Sponsors," *Financial Analysts Journal* 65, no. 6 (November/December 2009): 34–51. They estimated the annual costs to be in excess of $300 billion.
4. See Amit Goyal and Sunil Wahal, "The Selection and Termination of Investment Management Firms by Plan Sponsors," *Journal of Finance* 63, no. 4 (August 2008): 1805–1847.
5. Social scientists have recognized a problem called Ettore's Law against changing lines when queuing for service. Most of us recognize the "tellers' line irony": you change lines at the bank only to see your prior line somehow speed up just as your new line seems to slow down.

6. Amazingly, even some index funds charge high fees—as much as 75 basis points—for an S&P 500 matching fund.

7. See David F. Swensen, *Unconventional Success: A Fundamental Approach to Personal Investment* (New York: Free Press, 2005).

8. As Bing Crosby once crooned, they would "accentuate the positive, eliminate the negative" and not "mess with Mr. In-Between."

9. The payouts to sellers have also become large—unless you think $1 billion for a first-generation service proprietorship is not large.

10. One explanation for the shift away from counseling by investment managers may be that as institutions used more numerous and more specialized investment managers, they apparently wanted to separate the two functions and have independent investment consultants monitor the managers just as outside auditors monitor financial reporting.

RECOMMENDED READING

IF YOU WISH TO READ MORE, AS I HOPE YOU WILL, HERE ARE 10 choices you'll find both enjoyable and worthwhile.

1. *Berkshire Hathaway Annual Reports.* Warren Buffett, widely recognized as our most successful investor, explains with some humor and much candor what he and his partner Charlie Munger are doing—and why. Delightful as recreational reading and profoundly instructive, these remarkable annual reports are an open classroom for all investors. The justly famous annual meetings of Berkshire's stockholders are equally candid, entertaining, and informative. Current and past years' reports are available at berkshirehathaway.com.

2. *The Intelligent Investor* by Benjamin Graham, the acknowledged founder of the profession of investment management. This is an "advanced primer." Jason Zweig, deservedly one of the most popular commentators on investing, has published a shrewdly annotated edition (Harper Collins Business Essentials) full of contemporary insights and perspective. If you want more depth, breadth, and rigor, turn to *Security Analysis* (McGraw-Hill), which is often simply called

"Graham and Dodd" after its authors. For 80 years, through six editions, it has been the professional investor's bible.

3. *Tap Dancing to Work* (Portfolio Penguin) is Carol Loomis's annotated collection of the many articles on or by her long-time friend Warren Buffett that have appeared in *Fortune*.

4. *John Bogle on Investing: The First 50 Years* (McGraw-Hill). Jack Bogle is the tribune for the individual investor, the founder of Vanguard, and a crusader who thinks clearly, writes well, and has a lot to say that we can all treasure and use.

5. *Pioneering Portfolio Management* (Free Press). David F. Swensen, Yale University's remarkably successful chief investment officer, explains how to manage a large tax-exempt portfolio in a thoroughly modern way, with no jargon, no complex equations, and lots of good thinking and judgment. Fully accessible to serious amateurs, this is the best book ever written about professional investing. Swensen's thoughtful and explicit explanation of the reasoning behind each aspect of Yale's endowment clearly invites—even obliges—every other institution to develop its own answers to each of these core questions:

- What is your strategic portfolio structure and *why*?
- How do you select investment managers and *why*?
- What is your spending rule and *why*?
- What are your investment committee's particular functions and responsibilities and *why*?

6. *Thinking, Fast and Slow* (Farrar, Straus and Giroux) presents Daniel Kahneman's engaging explanation of the work he and other leading behavioral economists have done to show that our behavior is not nearly as rational as economists used to believe *and* that our irrational behaviors are remarkably consistent and predictable.

7. *The Crowd* by Gustave Le Bon (Dover Publications). This book, first published long ago, shows that intelligent people

lose their rationality and individuality when they join groups or, worse, become part of a crowd. Investors exhibit "crowd behavior" all too often, creating bubbles and panics.

8. *The Only Investment Guide You'll Ever Need* by Andrew Tobias (Mariner Books) is an easy-reading primer without any patronizing. It is clear, comprehensive, candid, and charming. No wonder it has sold over 1.5 million copies.

9. *A Random Walk Down Wall Street* by Burton Malkiel (W. W. Norton). Having also sold over 1.5 million copies, this popular and engaging guide to what the professionals know—and all investors *should* know—tells all about the best and most useful research and how to unlock its power in your investing life. This book is straight talk from one of Princeton's all-time favorite professors.

10. *The Investor's Anthology* (John Wiley & Sons) is a collection of seminal articles of great influence, with justly famous insights and ideas that "ring the bell" for professional investors.

11. *The Index Revolution* (John Wiley & Sons) tells how, as the market changed in many major ways yours truly went from being an active investor to an indexer. Any investor who is not yet indexing should read this compelling case for indexing—and then decide.

12. *The Elements of Investing* by Burton G. Malkiel and Charles D. Ellis (John Wiley & Sons) is a short clear guide to investing that meets all the real needs of a beginner—in less than two hours of easy reading.

INDEX

ABOUT THE AUTHOR

Charles D. Ellis founded and served for three decades as managing partner of Greenwich Associates, the global leader in strategy consulting to professional financial service firms. There he consulted with the world's leading investment managers and securities firms in North America, Asia, and Europe. The author of 17 books and well over 100 articles on investing and finance, Ellis has taught advanced investment courses at both Harvard Business School and the Yale School of Management. His path-breaking paper "The Loser's Game," published in the *Financial Analysts Journal,* won the profession's Graham and Dodd Award for excellence in 1975. In addition to chairing CFA Institute, the investment management profession's worldwide association, and being one of only a dozen leaders honored for lifetime contributions to the investment profession, Ellis has served as a trustee of Phillips Exeter Academy, an overseer of the Stern School of Business at New York University, a trustee and chair of the finance committee of the Robert Wood Johnson Foundation, a director of Vanguard, and successor trustee and, for many years, chair of the investment committee of Yale University. He is chairman of the Whitehead Institute for Biomedical Research.

In recent years, Ellis has served as an advisor to large institutional funds and investors in Australia, New Zealand, Singapore, Vietnam, Saudi Arabia, the United Kingdom, Qatar, Canada, and the United States. His most recent book, *The Index Revolution,* also published by John Wiley & Sons, explains how major changes in investment management and securities markets over five decades have inevitably made indexing increasingly compelling for all investors.